WHEN DINOSAURS RULED THE SCREEN

By Marc Shapiro

IMAGE
PUBLISHING

ALSO From Image Publishing:

- Above & Below: A Guide to Beauty and the Beast
- Dark Shadows in the Afternoon
- Trek Classic: 25 Years Later
- The Making of the Trek Films
- New Voyages: The Next Generation Guidebook
- Night Stalking: A 20th Anniversary Kolchak Companion
- The Animated Films of Don Bluth
- Time Tripping: A Guide to Quantum Leap

ALSO By the Same Author:

- Newcomers Among Us: The Alien Nation Companion
- The Vampire Interview Book: Conversations With the Undead

When Dinosaurs Ruled the Screen is published by Image Publishing of New York. Reproduction by any means is strictly prohibited without prior written permission. All correspondence should be addressed to Image Publishing, 2083 Hempstead Turnpike, Suite 150, East Meadow, New York 11554.

Book Design by Perfect Pages. Cover Design by Paul Nicosia.

First Printing, First Edition: March 1992
Printed in the United States of America

ISBN#0-9627508-0-2

Dedicated To:

Bennie Shapiro (1924-1964), for taking me to my first monster movie, *Invaders From Mars*, in 1953. Thanks, Dad.

Freda Ellinwood (1917-1990), for putting the lie to every mother-in-law story ever told.

Nancy and Rachael Shapiro, for their love, support and for putting up with my mania for things that go bump in the night.

AUTHOR'S ACKNOWLEDGEMENTS: The author would like to thank the following people for their time and memories: Ray Harryhausen, Bert I. Gordon, Ray Bradbury, Ib Melchior, Fred Freiberger, David Allen, Bill Stout, Steve Miner and David Gerrold.

An additional thank you to *Starlog* and *Fangoria* magazines, and the books *The Making of King Kong*, *Keep Watching the Skies*, *The Girl in the Hairy Paw* and *The Animated Films of Don Bluth*, whose invaluable information and insights made research a pleasure. And, finally, thanks to Forrest J. Ackerman and Dickens Videos, for your nuts-and-bolts help.

An Introduction

When the MILLION $ MOVIE aired the original GODZILLA nine times in one week, I saw GODZILLA nine times in one week. CHILLER THEATRE's umpteenth showings of THE GIANT BEHEMOTH and THE BEAST FROM HOLLOW MOUNTAIN? I had a front-row seat. When our junior high school "noon movie" program had the infinite wisdom to run GORGO in five thrilling installments, life suddenly became worth living. I had the Dinosaur "Jones" in the worst way. And, happily, over the years I've discovered that I was not alone.

Tyrannosaurus Rex!

Brontosaurus!

Triceratops!

Megalosaurus!

The names scream fear and fascination, appeal and imagination. There is something about names that appear cast in 40-foot high base relief that strikes at something very primitive, very childlike and very exciting in all of us.

And, in the immortal words of paleontologist Peter Dodson, "If dinosaurs did not exist, we would have invented them.

Dinosaurs did exist. The evidence of their life and their passing through our timeline   is on display for all to see. But the fact that   they *did* exist has not stopped Hollywood   from reinventing these fabulous

creatures in motion pictures that run the gamut from the ridiculous (KING DINOSAUR and VARAN THE UN-BELIEVABLE) to the sublime (KING KONG, THE VALLEY OF GWANGI and THE BEAST FROM 20,000 FATHOMS) and all points in between.

The fascination with putting dinosaurs on the big screen is something that just won't go away. After the rather lean decade of the 80's in which BABY....SECRET OF THE LOST LEGEND and CAVEMAN were the only two brushes with prehistoric cinema, the 90's appear headed full throttle back to the Cretaceous.

A number of films with dinosaurs at their core are in various stages of production and release. But leave it to Steven Spielberg to give this long respected genre the 90's legitimacy it craves with the recent announcement that JURASSIC PARK, the film adaptation of the Michael Crichton novel about DNA cloned dinosaurs on the prowl, will soon be going into production for a tentative 1993 release.

And when Spielberg steps up to take his turn at letting dinosaurs rule the

screen, he'd better be on his best creative behavior. Because Willis O'Brien, Ray Harryhausen, Ray Bradbury and countless other guardians of the dinosaur hall of fame will be looking over his shoulder—watching for that false step. The pet shop lizard with a fin glued on? A man in a rubber suit? The gods who have brought dinosaurs to center stage and the silver screen would not like that....

And neither would kids like me.

Marc Shapiro
December 1991

WHEN DINOSAURS RULED THE SCREEN

Table of Contents

1

The

Stone

Age

The cinematic age of dinosaurs began in 1909 when a friendly Brontosaurus crawled out of a cartoon cave to nuzzle a live action actress in a cartoon entitled GERDIE THE DINOSAUR. It was a modest, albeit childish, first step but, like all good first steps, it kicked off a journey that continued—three years later—with the initial creaky attempt at filmdom's first "live" dinosaur movie.

Pioneering filmmaker D.W. Griffith had a passion for all things primitive. It resulted in the 1913 film, MAN'S GENESIS (a.k.a. IN PREHISTORIC DAYS and BRUTE FORCE). This short pitted cave men against prehistoric reptiles; in actuality an unconvincing alligator and snake done up in fake horns and other attachments designed to make them look like dinosaurs. What saves MAN'S GENESIS from being a totally disposable nugget of the silent era is a sequence in which a mock-up of a Ceratosaurus, in an early and only mildly convincing form of animation, moves briefly in and out of frame.

ON MOONSHINE MOUNTAIN, which followed in 1914, was another lizards as dinosaurs epic which featured intercut shots of dinosaurs and human actors, but not in the same frame. Still, this film did indicate that a good idea was taking root; an idea that was about to be improved upon by a cowboy-turned boxer-turned filmmaker named Willis O'Brien.

O'Brien, who had already experimented with stop motion animation by manipulating clay models in gradual, frame-at-a-time movements and photographing the results, decided to expand his horizons in 1914 by shooting 75 feet of untitled stop motion footage that featured a cave man and a Brontosaurus. This comic short brought much interest from the film community, but no firm offers.

Undaunted, O'Brien continued his stop motion fascination with dinosaurs, creating a one-reel comedy called THE DINOSAUR AND THE MISSING LINK in 1915. The movie, filmed over a two-month period in the basement of a San Francisco theatre, featured cave men, an ape-like missing link which O'Brien once jokingly described as "Kong's ancestor" and a Brontosaurus. The film's thin storyline saw the missing link and the Brontosaurus in a deadly battle that ends with the dinosaur emerging victorious. While a slight entry into the dinosaur derby, THE DINOSAUR AND THE MISSING LINK did showcase a further refinement of the stop motion process in which jointed wooden skeletons were covered with clay and then sculpted.

THE DINOSAUR AND THE MISSING LINK was purchased and distributed by the New York-based Thomas A. Edison Company, whose president enticed O'Brien to come aboard to make more dinosaur comedies under a newly created subsidiary called Mannikin Films. Under that banner, O'Brien churned out such one-reel wonders as R.F.D. 10,000 B.C., PREHISTORIC POULTRY and CURIOUS PETS OF OUR ANCESTORS. All of these short films stuck to a rigid formula that featured puppet cave men and prehistoric animals put through primitive stop motion paces. But O'Brien, ever the experimental soul, managed to push the envelope on the short movie SAM LOYD'S FAMOUS PUZZLES —THE PUZZLING BILLBOARD AND NIPPY'S NIGHTMARE as the first film to combine live action and animated sequences.

But while making great strides, O'Brien was also growing frustrated at Hollywood's unwillingness to move beyond caricature to a more authentic depiction of dinosaurs on screen. A deal for an educational film series, which would have allowed O'Brien to show dinosaurs as reality-based creatures, was developed but subsequently fell through. For him it was the first of many dinosaur related disappointments as remembered by Ray Harryhausen, O'Brien's student and famed stop motion animator.

"He had a lot of problems," says Harryhausen. "He was the only one doing these kinds of effects at the time and he had a lot of trouble trying to convince people that these things could work the way he wanted them to work. He had so many projects fall through before they reached the screen. How he survived all those disappointments I'll never know."

O'Brien licked his wounds and soon found a kindred spirit in film technician Herbert M. Dawley, who, likewise, wanted to portray dinosaurs as real. The pair entered into a deal in 1919 to produce THE GHOST OF SLUMBER MOUNTAIN, a lightweight mystery/adventure in which one Uncle Jack chronicles his adventures on Slumber Mountain and Dream Valley at the insistence of his nephews. In the story, Uncle Jack stumbles upon the haunted cabin of Mad Dick, whose ghost appears and gives him an instrument that allows him to see the area as it was millions of years ago. It is at this point that the film's dinosaur action, an Allosaurus fighting a Triceratops and attempting to chow down on Uncle Jack, takes place. But before Jack can become dinosaur stew, he wakes up and we discover that THE GHOST OF SLUMBER MOUNTAIN was only a dream.

O'Brien, working in conjunction with vertebrate paleontologist Dr. Barnum Brown, constructed five life-like dinosaurs for SLUMBER MOUNTAIN and was true to his vision of not presenting them in slapstick fashion. His approach to animating his creations consisted of photographing miniature dinosaurs against miniature sets and matching them with full scale scenes of human actors. The results received rave reviews from both the film and scientific community when the movie was released by World Cinema that same year.

"I was greatly pleased," said Dr. G. Clyde Fisher of the American Museum of Natural History after viewing the film. "It's astonishing how lifelike those old dinosaurs were. The whole thing was extremely well done."

The success of THE GHOST OF SLUMBER MOUNTAIN brought O'Brien in contact with a long-time fan of his work, Watterson R. Rothacker, president of the Chicago-based Rothacker Film Company. O'Brien was hired by him to create yet another series of dinosaur one-reelers, but both filmmakers soon made the leap to higher ground when Rothacker secured the film rights to Sir Arthur Conan Doyle's THE LOST WORLD.

THE LOST WORLD follows a group of explorers, headed by the flamboyant professor Challenger, up the Amazon River to an isolated plateau where they encounter live dinosaurs. After a series of adventures that has the group fighting off the advances of an Allosaurus, Brontosaurus and others, they capture a live Brontosaurus and return with it to London. There the beast accidently escapes and lays waste to much of the city, before ultimately swimming out to sea.

O'Brien, ever the realist, recognized that to properly interpret the scope and detail of Doyle's tale would tax the limits of what had been, to that point, essentially a one-man operation. A deal was subsequently struck to co-produce the film with First National Pictures, which beefed up the effects arsenal with the addition of that company's

Fred Jackman. But the stop motion pioneer knew that the tools that had served him so well on one-reel comedies and short features—namely clay, cloth and wood—would not do justice to the wide array of monsters present in Doyle's world. O'Brien felt he would need a sculptor with special vision to help him with the project, and he soon discovered one in the person of Otis Art Institute student Marcel Delgado. Delgado was initially reluctant to give up the security of his job as a $14.00 a week grocery clerk for the uncertainty of the motion picture business. In THE MAKING OF KING KONG, he recalled what O'Brien did to make him change his mind.

"Mr. O'Brien said why don't you take a day off from work and visit me at the studio. I could not turn down the offer to see pictures being filmed so I went to the studio. After the tour of the different sets, he took me to his studio that was filled with pictures and models of dinosaurs. O'Brien said, 'Well Marcel, how do you like your studio? It's all yours if you want it.' He asked when can you start? I replied right now."

Delgado spent the next two years creating an estimated 50 miniature dinosaur models. His dinosaur army, which included Allosaurus, Brontosaurus, Stegosaurus and others, were modeled after the classic Charles R. Knight paintings. But the innovation of Delgado and O'Brien's LOST WORLD creations went quite literally below the skin.

The original Lost World

The 18-inch skeletons were constructed to include ball and socket joints and articulated backbones that allowed for movable digits and appendages. Skins were made of latex and rubber sheeting. Some of the dinosaurs contained air bladders that, when activated off camera, gave the creatures the appearance of breathing. The attention given to bringing these monsters to life was, by silent era standards, amazing.

In 1922, O'Brien produced the first "test footage" of THE LOST WORLD dinosaurs in motion. This film made the rounds and was universally applauded by no lesser light than Arthur Conan Doyle himself. Finally, after six and a half years of preparation, First National announced, in 1924, that THE LOST WORLD was in active production at a budget in excess of $1 million. Directing the live action sequences was Harry O. Hoyt, with William Dowling handling second unit. Heading the cast were such top stars of the era as Wallace Beery, Lewis Stone, Bessie Love, Lloyd Hughes and Bull Montana.

While sets representing the streets of London and jungle and plateau exteriors were no less impressive, the lion's share of attention during THE LOST WORLD's production focused on the dinosaur sequences. The scenes in which the explorers witness dinosaur battles or are chased, were staged on a 300-foot stage that was designed to give the miniatures a look of prehistoric size. The animation sequences were shot with seven dolly-mounted cameras whose shutters were operated from a single control. O'Brien accomplished the feat of featuring dinosaurs and live actors in the same frame of film by masking off portions of the film negatives, photographing the actors against a matching background and inserting that shot into the masked off portion of the frame.

One of the most spectacular sequences in THE LOST WORLD occurs at film's end when the Brontosaurus crushes London underfoot. The scenes were accomplished through a very early form of travelling matte camera work. The dinosaur was animated against a white background and created as both a negative and positive image. Both images were then inserted into the masked portions of frames containing the city and people running. Playing off of dinosaurs that were not there proved quite the acting challenge for those involved in the film.

"When the prehistoric monsters started chasing us, Mr. Hoyt would take us aside and explain to us that there were terrifying creatures and that we should be scared to death of them," recalled actress Bessie Love in her autobiography. "Then he would yell action and we would look terrified and scamper from dinosaurs that were not even on the stage."

THE LOST WORLD was released in 1925 and was a critical and box office smash. So much so that a sequel was immediately announced that would have Hoyt and O'Brien reteaming in a story that, according to the first film's production manager Earl Hudson, "would be en-tirely different from the original."

The sequel rumor persisted into 1928 but, with the onset of talkies, interest in dinosaur movies waned and THE LOST WORLD follow up was abandoned. But Hollywood was cyclical even in the old days and so, in 1930, it did not come as too much of a surprise when it was announced that O'Brien and Hoyt were reteaming for a dinosaur epic called CREATION.

CREATION told the story of a group of explorers who travel by submarine to a huge promontory which has risen up out of the sea during an earthquake. The submarine is destroyed and our intrepid group soon finds itself fighting for their lives amid a literal who's who of dinosaurs, that includes Brontosaurus, Tyrannosaurus Rex, Stegosaurus, Triceratops, Pterodactyl and others. At the film's end, a volcano erupts, dinosaurs stampede and all seems lost until a rescue helicopter arrives and flys the survivors to safety just as the island explodes.

RKO Pictures, who agreed to produce the film, liked CREATION's action-adventure tone. What they failed to realize was that the technology required to make a dinosaur movie had advanced quite a bit since THE LOST WORLD and would therefore be much more expensive.

O'Brien, once again aided by Marcel Delgado, set about creating a new generation of stop motion beasts. Animation for sound pictures now required 24 frames per second of screen time rather than silent film's 16 frames per second. But that eight frame difference translated into a much longer animation period. O'Brien and a crew that was learning the process of the job labored through 1930 and 1931. Twenty seconds of usable footage a day was considered an outstanding day's work. But, despite some notable test footage of the island rising from the sea, the submarine being destroyed and a Triceratops goring an explorer to death, a new executive regime at RKO decided that a movie that had already run up over $100,000 in expenses on only a few feet of film, would ultimately end up costing too much and pulled the plug on CREATION.

But the death of CREATION had a silver lining in it for Willis O'Brien. RKO's money man, Merian Cooper, while pronouncing the death sentence on CREATION, saw the potential for O'Brien and his dinosaurs in a little project that had been on his creative backburner for a long time.

That project was KING KONG.

2

The
Big
Ape

KING KONG was about a giant ape and the beauty who ultimately brought him crashing to earth. But you would have to search pretty far afield to find a better supporting cast than the variety of Mesozoic nasties Kong did battle with on Skull Island.

While the first question KING KONG producer Merian Cooper had for Willis O'Brien was "Can you build a better ape?", O'Brien's reputation as the dean of dinosaurs was not lost on him. Cooper, in the book THE MAKING OF KING KONG, dismissed CREATION's footage as "just a lot of animals walking around." But animation legend Ray Harryhausen recalls that much of that film's dinosaur sequences found their way into the KING KONG script.

"The Pteranodon carrying the girl away was in the CREATION script," lists Harryhausen. "The Arsinotherium knocking the men off the log was in CREATION and was in KING KONG until the producers decided to have Kong roll the log. In CREATION, the Brontosaurus came up under a boat. In KING KONG it came up under a raft."

KING KONG had been germinating in the minds of Cooper and the film's eventual director, Ernest B. Schoedsack, since 1927. Their initial take on the film was to feature a man in a gorilla suit and Komodo dragon lizards as the dinosaurs. The story, which at one point in pre-production went under the title THE BEAST, tells the tale of a film crew shooting on location on the mysterious Skull Island. The filmmakers discover a wall constructed by the natives to protect them from something mysterious that lives on the other side of the island; something called Kong.

During the night, actress Ann Darrow (Fay Wray) is kidnapped by the natives and tied to a sacrificial alter; the better to become the bride of Kong. To everybody's surprise and horror, a giant ape arrives and takes the girl. The crew, headed by Carl Denham (Robert Armstrong) and John Driscoll (Bruce Cabot), gives chase and soon

Merian Cooper oversees the cast of "King Kong" (photo copyright © 1933 RKO)

encounter terrifying dinosaurs who succeed in killing most of the rescuers. Ann is finally rescued and Kong is captured and taken to New York, where he escapes and destroys much of the city before meeting his fate atop the Empire State Building.

KING KONG, in 1931, was considered risky business by RKO bigwigs. For this reason, when Cooper commissioned O'Brien to create a test reel of Kong and dinosaur footage to convince the studio of the feasibility of the project, he avoided a lot of unnecessary speculation by christening his effort the top secret "Project 601." Faced with getting maximum animation for minimum budget, O'Brien once again turned to Marcel Delgado, who supplemented his leftover CREATION models with new, larger scale Stegosaurus, Allosaurus, Pterodactyls and other prehistoric reptiles.

Much of O'Brien's animation work on KING KONG would be done by matching live action footage with miniatures and models in much the same way as was done on THE LOST WORLD. But as he and his veteran crew would discover, the animating of the movie would result in their pushing the special effects envelope.

Animation in previous O'Brien adventures had been relatively simple, predicated on the fact that most of his dinosaurs operated on a fixed axis of movement. The creatures of Skull Island, on the other hand, would be required to showcase rapid walking and running.

O'Brien met the task with a specially constructed table top set that had holes drilled through its base. Into these holes were inserted clamps that would anchor themselves into the metal feet of the models to keep them stable as they were manipulated in frame-at-a-time steps.

O'Brien's formidable animation task was made easier with the discovery—about the time the test reel was being created—of a variation of the, to that point, accepted form of rear screen projection. Rear projection in the past had always been plagued by unsteady synchronization between the screen projecting the background image and the camera shooting the image and the actors in front of it. A refinement of the screen, credited to RKO technician Sidney Saunders, would now allow KING KONG's animators to avoid the problems of hot spots and unnecessary screen movement, and project a cleaner rear projection image in to the camera.

Learning the ins and outs of this new process proved an arduous task that often saw cast and crew working 20 hours a day to match live action with dinosaur footage being shot by O'Brien on a faraway miniature table. As for the animation itself, O'Brien saw fit to use wooden figures, in lieu of leftover CREATION dinosaurs and newer models, in the early test stages. The detail that he brought to even his preliminary sequences is highlighted by the fact that he would expose a few feet of film for every one frame, develop and blow up those frames and use them to align both light and movement to his specifications.

O'Brien's assessment of the challenges he faced and conquered on KING KONG were covered in the book THE GIRL IN THE HAIRY PAW, where he said, "The completed shots represented the ultimate in applied talents creating the ultimate picture. Each scene was planned as a single picture, a dramatic conception in black and white."

His test reel—10 minutes of film containing 147 scenes—was finally screened for RKO executives in 1932. The dinosaur-involved scenes included Kong fighting and killing the Tyrannosaurus Rex, the Brontosaurus rising out of the water and capsizing the raft, Kong fighting a Pterodactyl and an outtake from CREATION in which a Triceratops chases and kills a man. Reception to the footage was mixed, but Cooper's insistence and O'Brien's magic convinced RKO to go ahead with KING KONG that same year.

O'Brien immediately plunged into the Saunders rear projection refinement for the scene in which Ann (live action) screams as she watches Kong and the Tyrannosaurus Rex do battle. So taken with the idea was O'Brien that, during the course of filming, he developed a variation of the process that would function on a miniature setting. The animator's attention to detail added yet another facet in the aforementioned Kong vs Rex sequence.

King Kong and Friend (photo copyright © 1933 RKO)

Theorizing that Kong was far enough along the evolutionary line, his battles with the dinosaur would resemble a human boxing battle. O'Brien subsequently attended a number of boxing and wrestling matches, adapted specific holds and poses to the ape and worked them into the scene.

Making Kong's prehistoric counter-parts come alive became more complex and complicated as the production went on. A case in point is the relatively minor moment when the snake-like Elasmosaur emerges from the pool of water inside Kong's cave to attack Darrow and Driscoll. The creature emerging from real water was shot separately and matted into the existing frame. Another matte, this one of bubbling lava, was also cut into the frame. Steam photographed against a black velvet background followed as did the individually shot scene of the actors.

Adding to the already crowded frame were the stop motion models of Kong, the dinosaur and the models of the actors which were animated by O'Brien against a rear projected cave interior.

The effects man, in later years, would often cite the scene in which Kong battles the Pteranodon as the most difficult scenes in the movie. Once you get beyond the fact that it would have been physically impossible for the winged creature to carry of a full-sized human, it's easy to see O'Brien's reasoning. Not only does the reptile fly, it also flaps its wings furiously when it falls into the grasp of Kong. He accomplished this feat by suspending the Pteranodon model and patiently animating each wing beat and body movement. Coordinating the movements of the actors in that sequence was done through the use of animated mannequins in some parts of the scene and projected live action in others.

Giving voice to the Skull Island dinosaurs was a problem that kept Walter G. Elliot, head of the sound effects department at RKO, up nights until he broached the question of what the dinosaurs sounded like to J.W. Lytle, vertebrate paleontologist at the Los Angeles County Museum of Natural History. Lytle's response, as chronicled in a 1933 issue of POPULAR SCIENCE MONTHLY, was "For the dinosauria I would suggest you reproduce various degrees of hissing sounds."

Elliot took the suggestion to

Storyboard for the giant spider sequence in "King Kong" subsequently cut (photo copyright © 1933 RKO)

"Son of Kong" (photo copyright © 1933 RKO)

heart and the Tyrannosaurus soon had a distinct hiss; the combination of a puma call mixed with the steam sound from a compressed air machine. Sounds made by the Brontosaurus and other Skull Island denizens were a series of croaks and hisses, supplied by sound technicians who made the appropriate sounds into megaphones.

As KING KONG lumbered closer to its release date, it became evident that while RKO had a dyed-in-the-wool classic on its hands, it also had a movie that, commercially speaking, was 20-30 minutes too long. Something had to go and, unfortunately, when producer Cooper swung his axe, it was in the direction of O'Brien's creations. As a result, gone in the final cut of the film are the scenes in which Kong confronts a mother Triceratops and her young, one involving a Styracosaurus and the sequence that features the mammal Arsinoitherium.

KING KONG opened in the New Roxy and Radio City Music Hall in New York on March 2, 1933. The movie was an immediate hit. And to nobody's surprise, Merian Cooper, in announcing RKO's slate of 11 new pictures for the coming year, included an innocuous title

JAMBOREE, which listed KING KONG director Schoedsack at the helm. The film was, in reality, a smoke screen for SON OF KONG.

"We called it JAMBOREE to keep people from visiting the set," said Schoedsack in THE MAKING OF KING KONG. "If they had known we were making another Kong picture, they would have drove us crazy trying to find out how it was done."

SON OF KONG picks up the Kong trail in New York, where an impoverished and debt-ridden Carl Denham joins some new explorers and old Kong alumni on a return trip to Skull Island in search of lost treasure. Our group soon finds themselves face to fang with another set of dinosaurs and a smaller and friendlier great ape. The treasure is discovered just in time for the island to begin to sink into the ocean. Kong's offspring makes the ultimate sacrifice by holding Denham above the water until he can be rescued, the film's token bad guy devoured by a sea monster and everybody else living happily ever after. The film once again stars Robert Armstrong as Denham and Helen Mack as Hilda, the token damsel in distress.

SON OF KONG was a rush job; conceived primarily to cash in on the success of the original and, consequently, necessitated O'Brien and model maker Delgado's recycling some old friends as well as creating some new ones. Returning for a cameo from the original KING KONG is a Brontosaurus, which engages in a knockdown, drag-out with baby Kong near the film's conclusion. The Styracosaurus, which was cut out of the final version of KING KONG, shows up to chase the new generation of explorers. A pair of original Delgado creations, the results of O'Brien's order to "build something nobody has ever seen before," were a large dragon-like creature and the briefly seen but terrifying sea monster which rises up out of the ocean to chow down on the bad guy.

Lessons learned from the original KONG were brought into play in bringing this new batch of prehistoric beasts to life. Miniature rear projection was used in the scene in which our heroes are chased and cornered by the Styracosaurus. The sea monster sequence has the actor in a composite with the creature as it rises out of the water. Unfortunately a rushed production schedule resulted in what many feel would have been O'Brien's master work, a full blown stampede of dinosaurs, being cut from the script.

SON OF KONG opened in 1933 and survived the stigma of being a sequel to an original of classic proportions, and managed to do good box office in the US and overseas. O'Brien, while happy with his work in the film, was not as enamored with the overall product.

The success of SON OF KONG did inspire Merian Cooper to go back to the well one more time with a third King Kong picture, actually a prequel to the original in which Kong leaves the island for an adventure on uncharted shores. This proposed third film never got beyond the imagining stages, but in 1939, Cooper, O'Brien and Delgado once again teamed up for a dinosaur-laced epic that would have made King Kong pale by comparison. The project was called WAR EAGLES.

WAR EAGLES told the tale of a group of natives living in a prehistoric world, who ride giant eagles and do battle with such dinosaurs as Tyrannosaurus Rex and Triceratops. At one point in the WAR EAGLES odyssey, the tribe wings its way to New York where our winged warriors do battle with modern day zeppelins.

The film got far enough along the development path that Delgado was set to work on creating a T-Rex and eagle models, which O'Brien used for some test footage. But interest in the project eventually waned and the decade of the 30's ended the way it had begun—with another dinosaur movie dead on arrival.

3

"It's a Screwy Idea For a Film"

Producer-director Hal Roach had an idea for a Stone Age Romeo and Juliet which would involve the rock people and the shell people, include dinosaurs, erupting volcanos and dialogue that would consist of grunts and gibberish. He knew that what he had in the storyline would become ONE MILLION B.C.

"It's a screwy idea for a film," deadpanned Roach in an interview prior to the start of production. He was right, but it was a screwy idea that seemed to hold some intriguing possibilities.

Victor Mature and Carol Landis as the lovesick Tomack and Luana appeared an interesting/oddball coupling. Lon Chaney Jr.'s

first foray into fantasy films didn't hurt either. And the idea of telling the story as a flashback paid a certain homage to the silent era that was unusual to say the least.

What seemed a more unusual move was Roach's hiring of famed director D.W. Griffith, who had been inactive for more than a decade, to work on the film. Now,

The original "One Million B.C." man against lizard

This is NOT King Kong and Godzilla doing the Tango in "Unknown Island".

here's where things start to get interesting!

Griffith, in numerous interviews, claimed he did, in fact, direct ONE MILLION B.C., the directing credit of which is given to Hal Roach Jr. In hindsight, there is much to the visual style of the film that indicates Griffith may well have had some hand in the filmmaking process. Roach, who it has been rumored got the idea for ONE MILLION B.C. from the much earlier Griffith silent movie, MAN'S GENESIS, said on many occasions that Griffith was only hired as a

consultant and general assistant. It was never his intention to let Griffith direct. Whether or not he actually directed any or all of Roach's prehistoric epic remains a mystery to this day.

What is not a mystery in the making of ONE MILLION B.C. is that Griffith did work in the special effects department, supervising what were known around the set as "the lizard shots." Which allows one to realize just how well dinosaurs fared in the film.

Dinosaur-wise, the long and

short of ONE MILLION B.C. is a mixed bag. Monitor lizards and crocodiles, worked into rear screen projection and matte paintings and blown to—well, dinosaur—size, comprised the lion's share of the creature work. While the effects were better than average for 1940, they were a definite step backward following a decade that saw O'Brien strut his stuff in KING KONG.

The effects worked a shade better in the scene in which a cave child is attacked by an Allosaurus. The creature, a man in a suit, was photographed in an effective array of long shots and extreme close-ups among trees and other shrubbery which masked the monster's shortcomings, while adding to the sequence's visual style.

ONE MILLION B.C. was released in 1940, and while the jury still remains divided on the true worth of this film, even the most hardened critical hearts seem to have mellowed to the film's naive charm.

This was the only dinosaur movie attempted for much of the decade of the '40s, although Willis O'Brien tried to get a dinosaur verses cowboys adventure called GWANGI off the ground. This effort was given a cursory look by the studios and O'Brien cohort Marcel Delgado even went so far as to create an Allosaurus model for the occasion. But, like previous ideas, O'Brien's GWANGI fell to the wayside.

"One of the problems with Willis' getting GWANGI off the ground was that the animation required for the dinosaurs would take too long," reflects Ray Harryhausen, who would finally make O'Brien's GWANGI a reality in 1969 with THE VALLEY OF GWANGI. "These were the war years and studios wanted to get the pictures made and into theatres in as little time as possible. Stop motion animation took too much time for them."

That process was nowhere to be found in the decade's only other dinosaur entry, UNKNOWN ISLAND. This 1948 quickie, which stars Richard Denning, Virginia Grey and Barton MacLaine, focuses on a man and woman who head up an expedition to an island to investigate strange creatures seen from the air during World War II. Once on the island, the group comes face-to-face with some of the worst dinosaur effects ever committed to film. To wit, Brontosaurus models being pulled by strings through miniature jungle scenes; men in Tyrannosaurus Rex suits limping through a desert sequence; and, in a case of near-ludicrous proportions, a man in a gorilla suit masquerading as a giant ground sloth.

Taking the credit/blame for UNKNOWN ISLAND are director Jack Bernhard and a special effects department headed by Howard A. Anderson and Ellis Burman. Contrary to the popular critical drubbing the film continues to take, Denning, in a recent STARLOG interview with Tom Weaver and Michael Brunas, said, "The special effects in the film fascinated me. I felt that, for the time, the special effects were excellent."

A lean dinosaur decade gave way to the end of World War II and the beginning of the atomic age. Dinosaurs anyone? You bet!

4

Love Me, Love My B's

The last thing people expected out of the "I Like Ike" era of the 1950's was a literal tidal wave of dinosaur movies. But the combination of Cold War paranoia, coupled with the specter of the bomb hanging over our heads, inexplicably turned Hollywood in the direction of our prehistoric past. The result was no fewer than 13 dinosaur related films, and the batting average of those fossilized treats was pretty good.

Those fabulous '50s produced one certified classic, one or two overlooked gems, a Japanese import of monstrous proportions that started a genre of its own, as well as the expected sludge. The "B" level epics, in particular, were all over the landscape. Some were highly watchable, while some . . . well, you get the picture.

First out of the block was TWO LOST WORLDS (1950), which is not so much a dinosaur film as it is a low budget pirate swashbuckler featuring James Arness as the good guy who rescues the damsel in distress. Said distress reaches

"The Lost Continent" (photo copyright © 1951 Lippert Pictures, Inc.)

More magnified lizards and their victims in "King Dinosaur" (photo copyright © 1955 Lippert Pictures)

prehistoric heights when Arness and company are shipwrecked on a desert island and must face the horrors of ONE MILLION B.C. stock footage of everybody's favorite lizards fighting it out one more time.

At least the dinosaurs looked like dinosaurs in THE LOST CONTINENT (1951), a LOST WORLD style adventure in which a group of scientists climb a giant plateau in search of the top secret contents of a lost missile. What they discover is a green-tinted prehistoric world populated by stop motion animated Brontosaurs and Triceratops, a macho girl who helps our stalwart heroes out, a Russian spy and a token volcanic eruption that sends the scientists, minus the inevitable casualties, scrambling down the mountainside.

The dinosaur highpoints in this Sam Newfield directed low budgeter include a Brontosaurus treeing a scientist and two Triceratops fighting, with a scientist being gored by the victor. The animation, which also includes a giant lizard or two, is a step below O'Brien's efforts as evidenced by the slow and limited movements of the stop motion models.

If there is a real memorable element to THE LOST CONTINENT it is the cast, a literal who's who of '50s character actors that includes Cesar Romero, Chick Chandler, Sid Melton, Hugh Beaumont, John Hoyt and Whit Bissell. Hoyt, in a FANGORIA interview

Monkey plus diving helmet equals "Robot Monster" (photo copyright © Astor Pictures Corp.)

with Tony Timpone, recalled, "The paper-mache mountain we climbed in that film was set up right in the middle of the soundstage. We climbed that mountain for weeks to get to those dinosaurs."

THE JUNGLE (1952), like TWO LOST WORLDS, has only a nodding acquaintance with ancient animals. This jungle morality play, starring Rod Cameron, Cesar Romero and Marie Windsor, follows a group of explorers in search of live Mammoths in the wilds of India. The Mammoths—in reality slow moving elephants with fur coats glued on them—don't show up until the final few minutes of the film and are promptly dispatched by a landslide. In the interim, we are treated to '50s style lust, betrayal and shady dealings.

ROBOT MONSTER (1953), the classically bad misadventures of a one-ape (in a diving helmet no less) invasion of Earth, features George Nader and a ton of stock footage. Dinosaur enthusiasts should look for the quick snippet of giant lizard gunk in the sequences where the dreaded U-Ray is unleashed.

KING DINOSAUR (1955) is one of those magic moments in cinematic history: a film that wears its lower than low budget on its sleeve like a badge of honor and is ultimately so bad that, in a strange way, it is actually mildly amusing. The notorious Bert I. Gordon's entry into the film business, KING DINOSAUR tells the tale of a group of astronauts who land on the planet Nova where they are immediately set upon by rear projection Gila monsters, armadillos and iguanas a.k.a. dinosaurs. After endless chases and close calls, the astronauts, in their infinite wisdom, decide to blow up the planet with an atomic bomb (Hey! That's what I would have done).

Gordon, in hindsight, claims "that there's nothing really spectacular about the film. The budget was small. I'm talking really small. We knew going in that we were not going to be able to afford Willis O'Brien or Ray Harryhausen, and would have to use lizards."

And it was those lizards, and in particular the iguana that played King Dinosaur, who gave Gordon major headaches during what he remembers of the "under 30 day shoot" at Big Bear, California.

"We spent two days trying to get that damned lizard to move and it just wouldn't move. We thought it was dead. Finally, in desperation, I went to a library and

21

checked out a book on iguanas which said they would not move unless the temperature reached a certain level. So we brought in some heaters, put them next to the lizard and, presto, we had a live iguana. Those lizards basically dictated the action, but we were patient so eventually we got everything we wanted."

Producer-director Gordon, who went on to make bigger (although not always better) films, has a copy of every movie he ever made. Except, of course, KING DINOSAUR.

"I don't have a copy of that film," says Gordon. "And to be perfectly honest, I don't really want a copy."

ANIMAL WORLD (1955) is a documentary look at animal life from that budding disaster filmmaker of the future, Irwin Allen. The best thing about this oddity is the opening 10 minutes, which features Willis O'Brien designed and Ray Harryhausen animated dinosaurs foraging, fighting and finally

A dinosaur terrorizes a stuffed bull in "Beast of Hollow Mountain".

dying on some only-fair table top sets. The Brontosaurus, Ceratosaurus and Triceratops stop motion appears sluggish at times, but the film is worth a look for some of Harryhausen's earliest credited dinosaur work.

O'Brien's GWANGI idea finally found a home of sorts in 1956, when the production/directorial team of Edward Nassour and Ismael Rodriguez bought his idea of cowboys fighting dinosaurs and took it to Mexico, where it became THE BEAST OF HOLLOW MOUNTAIN, starring Guy Madison and Patricia Medina. The story is a bit slow kicking in, choking to a large degree on too much cattle ranch romance and treachery. Things do pick up in the second half as our T-Rex with an attitude begins to chow down on the locals. The final 10 minutes, in which Madison and the dinosaur do battle, showcases some surprisingly good, if not spectacular, action. Surprising considering that although the BEAST producers were wild about O'Brien's idea, they did not consider the stop motion

"The Land Unknown" (photo copyright © 1957 Universal Pictures)

pro for the job of animating the creature. What THE BEAST OF HOLLOW MOUNTAIN offers instead is a process hailed in ads as "Regalscope," in which a series of models are used in each frame to animate the creature's movements. While it's not O'Brien style animation, Regalscope, aided and abetted by some normal stop motion elements, holds up quite well, thank you.

THE LAND UNKNOWN (1957) was originally promoted by Universal Studios as a major science fiction event. It was to be in color, have major special effects and, rumor had it, Cary Grant was being talked up as the possible lead in this Jack Arnold directed adventure.

As these things often happen, however, Universal had a change of heart and withdrew the lion's share of the film's proposed budget. In short order, color became black and white, Cary Grant was replaced by the Universal stock company headed by Jock Mahoney, William Reynolds and Shawn Smith. And, when Jack Arnold left the project, the task of directing this suddenly scaled down lost world adventure fell into the hands of capable journeyman Virgil Vogel.

THE LAND UNKNOWN chronicles the adventures of a Navy/scientific expedition into the Antarctic, whose helicopter collides with a Pterodactyl and crash lands in a prehistoric valley some 3,000 feet below the snow line. Our plucky group finds itself fighting for survival against such supposedly long-dead denizens as a Tyrannosaurus Rex, which is slashed by the "business" end of the copter blades; an Elasmosaur and a long lost scientist from a previous expedition, who wants to trade a necessary aircraft part for the lady scientist so he can play Adam and Eve in his private Eden.

Given the miniscule budget, the dinosaurs, with the help of some atmospheric sets and matte paintings, come off better than they had any right to. Vogel, in a FANGORIA interview with Tom Weaver, offered the specifics of what made his dinosaur charge click.

"The Tyrannosaurus was a 12-foot high man in a suit, but all the man inside did was make it walk. The eyelid and mouth movements were all controlled by rubber hoses attached to a a hydraulic console offstage. The Elasmosaur was a model on railroad tracks set up under the pool we used for the lake. Its movements were also worked from a hydraulic console. The Pterodactyl was one of the cheapest things we had. It was a prop dangling from the end of a fishing pole."

The film, recalls the director, also boosted the low budget monster maker's best friend, monitor lizards blown up to dinosaur size. "I thought THE LAND UNKNOWN had some good special effects," insisted Vogel, "and the story was a great premise. I wish I could do it again now, knowing what I know about effects today."

It seemed inevitable that Roger Corman would eventually hop on board the prehistoric bandwagon, so nobody seemed too surprised when TEENAGE CAVEMAN (a.k.a. PREHISTORIC WORLD and OUT OF THE DARKNESS) screamed in and out of theatres in 1958. This stone age odyssey with a futuristic twist stars Robert Vaughn as a callow cave youth in search of knowledge, who discovers, to his horror, that Earth has been quite literally atom-blasted back to the stone age.

TEENAGE CAVEMAN boasts slim dinosaur pickings that consist of the stock giant lizard fight from ONE MILLION B.C. (Boy! How would you like a buck everytime that stuff turns up in another movie?) and some alleged unused lizard footage from that same film.

Vaughn winces at the memory of the film, calling it "one of the worst films ever made." Corman, on the other hand, "thinks it's a pretty good little movie." You be the judge.

Giant lizards haven't always been the basis for bad movies, as evidenced by JOURNEY TO THE CENTER OF THE EARTH (1959), that superior telling of the Jules Verne story starring James Mason, Arlene Dahl and Pat Boone. It features well-lit, well put together sequences at the center of the Earth, where our explorers are chased by giant lizards posing as dinosaurs. Rather than looking schlocky, that budgetary shortcut actually looks quite crisp and fits quite nicely with the quasi-cartoon nature of the film.

The up and down quality of B dinosaur movies during the decade

"Journey to the Center of the Earth" (photo copyright © 20th Century Fox)

ended on a relatively up note with THE GIANT BEHEMOTH (1959). BEHEMOTH begins in rather ominous fashion with the discovery of dead, and very radioactive, fish washing up on the English coastline. The cause? A prehistoric monster has been awakened from an oceanic sleep. In due course, the monster comes ashore and destroys London with radioactive heat and electric charges. The creature returns to the ocean where it is torpedoed into the after life by good guy dinosaur hunters Gene Evans and Andre Morrell.

The story? A not too subtle theft of the plotline of THE BEAST FROM 20,000 FATHOMS (to be discussed in a separate chapter), which was directed by Eugene Lourie. So guess who was hired to direct what was then considered the shooting script by Robert Abell and Allan Adler? You guessed it. Eugene Lourie.

"The original script for BEHEMOTH dealt with an invisible creature," Lourie told writer Paul Mandell. "But the distributors wanted something they could see and felt a prehistoric monster [in this case a fictitious Paleosaurus] would be just the ticket."

At that point, Lourie, along with writing partner Daniel Hyatt, took his BEAST FROM 20,000 FATHOMS script, rewrote it and, with few minor exceptions, it became the script that the director ultimately shot.

The production company originally wanted Ray Harryhausen to animate the title creature, but when Harryhausen was unavailable, they turned to his mentor Willis O'Brien. O'Brien, then 70, normally allowed a minimum of six months to create his stop motion effects. Budget and time considerations forced him to create his magic. To a certain extent, it shows.

The Behemoth's movements are very good; especially in the sequence in which the creature attacks a lighthouse and, later, knocks over major landmarks in

London. On the down side, the creature itself is not very distinctive looking and, if you look closely, you can see some of the model seams. The time squeeze also resulted in many sequences of destruction being eliminated from the script and, during filming, replaced with already used shots which were slightly disguised.

But BEHEMOTH, like its predecessor BEAST FROM 20,000 FATHOMS, presents moments of real threat and menace to an already familiar plotline. And talk about your classic shock endings, after ridding the world of the prehistoric nemesis, our heroes surface in their submarine only to hear a radio report that more dead fish have been reported washing up on U.S. shores.

A promise of more dinosaurs to come.

Genre great Willis O'Brien at work on "The Giant Behemoth" (photo copyright © 1959 Allied Artists)

"The Giant Behemoth" (photo copyright © 1959 Allied Artists)

5

Oh No! There Goes Tokyo

Time was when Godzilla meant business.

What probably comes to mind are such efforts as GODZILLA VS THE SMOG MONSTER, DE-STROY ALL MONSTERS, SON OF GODZILLA, GODZILLA VS ROCKY (just making sure you're paying attention).

But before Toho Films turned Godzilla, Rodan and some of their noble brethren into dinosaur drop-pings suitable for dull seven year olds and brain dead adults, Godzilla's doing the mash all over Tokyo was considered, for a relatively short time, a sacred film-making cause.

Godzilla and company doing the monster mash in "Destroy All Monsters" (photo copyright © Toho Films)

"Godzilla On Monster Island" (photo copyright © Downtown Distribution)

GODZILLA, KING OF THE MONSTERS (released as GOJIRA in Japan) was the brainchild of Japanese special effects man Eiji Tsuburay, a long time fan of the original KING KONG who wanted to create a creature that would rival the giant ape. With the aid of director Inoshiro Honda and screenwriter Takeo Murata (with a story supplied by Shigeru Kayama), Tsuburaya fashioned a tale that combined prehistoric monsters and the world's preoccupation with the possible dangers of atomic energy.

GOJIRA tells the story of a giant prehistoric animal laying dormant on the ocean floor, that has come to life as the result of the hydrogen bomb testing and is menacing residents on a small island off the coast of Japan. In short order, Godzilla, tiring of the slim pickings offered by fishing boats, wades ashore in downtown Tokyo and proceeds to destroy the city with brute strength and firebreathing, radioactive breath. He returns to his underwater lair, preparing for a final assault that

will most certainly level Tokyo and lead to the destruction of the rest of the world. All seems lost when into the fray steps the reclusive scientist, Dr. Serizawa, whose top secret experiment, the oxygen destroyer, is seen as the only solution to the Godzilla problem.

Serizawa is reluctant to release the destructive potential of his creation, but is finally convinced and, in a final dramatic underwater confrontation, releases the device, which turns Godzilla into a skeleton and, finally, to dust. Serizawa

(photo copyright © 1956 Trans World)

then cuts his air hose, committing a classic suicide that paves the way for his assistants, Ogata and Emiko, to live happily ever after.

GOJIRA was far from an original idea, but what the film lacked in originally it more than made up for in characterization, superior special effects and a never flagging tone of somber serious mindedness.

The strong Japanese cast, headed by veterans Akira Takarada and Takaashi Shimura, takes this all very seriously. Takarada, as Serizawa, is particularly strong,

reflecting the pain of his Kamikaze past and doing the noble thing in his relationship with the respectful Emiko.

Whether by design or budget limitations, GOJIRA's matching of miniature and models of Tokyo with the oversized man-in-a-suit Godzilla (played by Japanese stuntman Ryosaku Takasugi) work quite well and, when combined with Honda's deft handling of those black and white proceedings, presents a haunting, somberly stated adjunct to the story.

GOJIRA opened in Japan in 1954. Critically favorable reviews aroused interest on these shores and Trans World Films picked the film up for U.S. release. But, not willing to leave well enough alone, Trans World changed the film's title to GODZILLA, KING OF THE MONSTERS, edited out what they considered unnecessary scenes (many of which gave real insight into the character of Serizawa) and had director Terry Morse shoot some additional scenes involving actor Raymond Burr as American

Godzilla vs. Bionic Monster (photo copyright © Cinema Shares International)

reporter Steve Martin, who, according to the revamped storyline, while on assignment in Japan observes Godzilla's rampage (and adds a lure for American film audiences).

Producer-director Steve Miner, who claims he "got into the business because of the original GODZILLA," saw a pre-Raymond Burr version of the original Japanese cut, and offers that "it's a beautiful movie. There's this one scene of a survivor of Godzilla's first attack on Tokyo dying in a hospital that is very long, but very poetic. Well, when they added

Raymond Burr, they chopped that scene up, had a nurse from the original scene cut in so it appeared that she was talking to Burr. They added a double who obviously wasn't the same one in the original and they used lighting that was inferior to the lighting of the original."

GODZILLA, KING OF THE MONSTERS was released on these shores in 1956. The film duplicated its overseas success and, in the ensuing years, has gone on to become one of television's perennial attractions.

Meanwhile, back in Japan, the folks at Toho realized there was

gold in their big, green dinosaur and quickly put together a sequel called GOJIRA RAIDS AGAIN (1955). Godzilla had been reduced to atoms at the end of the first picture, so what was one to do? Just bring him back, call him Gigantis and pretend like the first film never happened!

For the record, GOJIRA RAIDS AGAIN finds Gigantis and a four-footed, spiky-backed dinosaur named Angorus fighting it out on a Japanese island. Both monsters fall into the sea and become separated. Angorus turns up in Tokyo and proceeds to stomp all over what-

"Rodan, the Flying Monster" (photo copyright © 1957 The King Brothers)

ever was left intact from the first film. Gigantis turns up and their fight begins anew. Gigantis, after what seems like an endless round of men-in-a-suit battles, kills Angorus and swims away at the fade.

GOJIRA RAIDS AGAIN was picked up for U.S. release, retitled GIGANTIS, THE FIRE MONSTER and released on these shores in 1959 to good but less than GODZILLA-like business. Toho put Godzilla out to pasture for the following six years,

but out of sight did not necessarily translate to out of mind. Especially in the United States, where the now long-defunct ABPT Pictures (and in particular producers Harry Rybnick, Ed Barison and Richard Kay) got the bright idea to do what amounted to a Godzilla-like film to go into production in America in 1957. Writers Ib Melchior and Ed Watson were commissioned to write this epic, which had the working title of THE VOLCANO MONSTERS.

"I'm sure this was the studio's response to the success of GODZILLA," recalls Melchior. "Ed and I were asked to write this monster thing and to basically Americanize the Godzilla movies."

The story given to Melchior and Watson by ABPT, and which the writer admits had more than a nodding acquaintance to GIGANTIS, THE FIRE MONSTER, centers on an expedition to a remote island that discovers two dinosaurs, a Tyrannosaurus Rex

"King Kong vs. Godzilla (photo copyright © 1963 Universal International)

and an Ankylosaur, in a state of suspended animation. The two creatures are put aboard an aircraft carrier bound for San Francisco.

On route, the Tyrannosaurus falls overboard. The aircraft carrier continues to San Francisco, were the Ankylosaur comes to life and begins having a fit at the city by the bay's expense. Meanwhile, the T-Rex, having good reptilian sense and being one hell of a swimmer, finds its way to San Francisco

where it renews an eons old feud with the other creature. San Francisco, needless to say, is trashed, the Ankylosaur is killed and the Tyrannosaurus jumps into the bay and swims off.

This is not a put on. Point of fact: THE VOLCANO MONSTERS was so much a go project that VARIETY, in its May 7, 1957 issue, announced that it was set to roll on June 17. The film, for whatever reason, never did but, like clockwork, GIGANTIS did reach theatres a year

and a half later. Melchior has a theory about this GIGANTIS/ VOLCANO MONSTERS mystery.

"I think the producers had seen the Japanese version of GIGANTIS, figured it would be released in the U.S., took the screenplay and said to Ed and I, 'Do this story.' Up until now, I had no idea that we might be redoing a Japanese script for an already completed movie."

Toho, in the meantime, was stretching its monster wings in a more literal sense with RODAN

(1957), in which giant flying reptiles stepped in for Godzilla. Rodan, directed by old hand Inoshiro Honda, begins in a mine as a pair of workers are attacked by giant bugs, the mine shaft collapses and the pair are presumed dead. One of the miners is discovered alive days later, and, in a delirious flashback, tells of seeing a giant bird hatch out of an egg in the deep bowels of the Earth and feed on the bugs.

Before you can say, "Oh, no, there goes Tokyo," not one but two giant Pterodactyls escape to the surface and begin picking off the locals as they fly by at supersonic speed. The giant reptiles soon wing their way to Japan's capital, where the city crumbles before the hurricane force winds generated by their wing speed. The army gives it their best shot, which, as usual, just isn't good enough. Just when things appear their darkest, a volcano erupts, trapping one of the monsters in its fiery breath. As the one giant reptile flutters into a lava flow, the other, not willing to live without its mate, joins in the fiery death.

RODAN, shot in color, has never been a critic's favorite but, like the original GODZILLA, has true strengths.

The early mine sequence are claustrophobic and rather creepy. The acting is better than average. The special effects and the expected miniatures for the city destruction are fairly realistic looking, and mobile models for the flying reptiles and bugs are fairly decent. The Rodans, unlike previous Toho

"Godzilla vs. The Thing" (photo copyright © Toho Films)

efforts, have no ties to the bomb. And the finale, despite its syrupy sermon on the mount narration, is quite dramatic.

The up and down quality of Toho's monster invasion took a definite downward spiral in 1958 when Honda went back to the well and came up with DAIKAIJU BARAN. The story is standard Toho simplicity. Experiments near a lake

brings forth the wrath of a thing that is a cross between Godzilla on a bad day and a flying squirrel. The creature flys around, menaces a local village and an airfield (but never gets within stomping distance of Tokyo, thank God) before being blown up by explosives flown in on the end of balloons.

The mush mind nature of the film took on an even deeper air of unbelievability when Crown International picked it up for U.S. release. The film was retitled VARAN THE UNBELIEVABLE and a total of 17 minutes (including all of the flying sequences) were cut. What was left was edited, shortened and—shades of GODZILLA—new scenes featuring B movie actor Myron Healy as a navy scientist who does battle with the monster, were shot and added.

As much of a goof as VARAN was, the film deserved brownie points for continuing the philosophy of deadly earnestness in all Toho monster efforts. Unfortunately, even that saving grace went by the boards when Godzilla came out of retirement in 1962 to do battle with a another giant of the silver screen in KINGU KONGU TAI GOJIRA, better known in America as KING KONG VS GODZILLA. Any sense of seriousness goes out the window as Kong is drugged and flown to Japan with the aid of a balloon. Godzilla, meanwhile, emerges from an iceberg and (surprise!) heads for Japan. Kong and Godzilla subsequently engage in some pathetic wrestling matches, throw boulders at each other, ignore the feeble Japanese army and fall off Mt. Fuji.

Kong appears to win in this one, but purists were so mad at this big ape in a suit that nobody seemed to care. The film's U.S. premiere in

"Godzilla vs. The Smog Monster (photo copyright © 1972 Toho Films)

1963 contained new scenes with American actor Michael Keith that neither helped nor hindered this bad joke of an exercise. What critics did not count on was this bad joke becoming the biggest grossing Toho film to date. Consequently, the next 12 Godzilla outings between 1964 and 1975 had the same elements in common: more bad monsters, declining special effects quality and an appeal to kids who weren't too swift. Rather than document each misadventure, the titles (Japanese titles in parenthesis) should suffice. The rest is up to you.

1964: GODZILLA VS THE THING (GODZILLA AGAINST MOTHRA), GHIDRAH, THE THREE HEADED MONSTER (the same); 1965: MONSTER ZERO (INVASION OF THE ASTRO MONSTERS); 1966: GODZILLA VS THE SEA MONSTER (EBIRAH, HORROR OF THE DEEP); 1967: SON OF GODZILLA (the same); 1968: DESTROY ALL MONSTERS (the same); 1969: GODZILLA'S REVENGE (the same); 1971: GODZILLA VS THE SMOG MONSTER (GODZILLA AGAINST HEDORA); 1972: GODZILLA ON MONSTER ISLAND (GODZILLA AGAINST GIGAN); 1973: GODZILLA VS MEGALON (GOZILLA AGAINST

"Son of Godzilla" (photo copyright © Toho Films)

"Godzilla's Revenge" (photo copyright © Toho Films)

MEGARO); 1974: GODZILLA VS THE BIONIC MONSTER, a.k.a. GODZILLA VS THE COSMIC MONSTER (GODZILLA VS MEKA-GODZILLA); 1975: TERROR OF GODZILLA, a.k.a. TERROR OF MEKA-GODZILLA (REVENGE OF MEKA-GODZILLA).

Godzilla once again went on an extended vacation in 1975 and would stay out of town until the mid 80's, but the spirit of his finest moments would always remain.

6

Classics From 20,000 Fathoms

THE BEAST FROM 20,000 FATHOMS was sneak previewed in a theatre in a small town just outside Los Angeles in 1953. People entering the theatre that night had no idea what they were going to see. One person who had more than an idea, BEAST co-writer Fred Freiberger, was also in attendance. Nobody recognizes the writer, so Freiberger felt secure in sneaking into the sneak to see people's reaction to the film first hand. He got his reaction alright, but not one that he expected.

"As soon as the creature appeared on the screen, mothers screamed, grabbed their children and ran out of the theatre," recalls Freiberger. "I was sitting there, watching all this and feeling a little ashamed. I had no idea what we had done or what we had created."

What the filmmakers intended was a modest, exploitable tale of a dinosaur brought back to life as a result of atomic testing, who trashes New York before meeting its end on the rollercoaster at Coney Island. What they ended up with, pure and simple, is a classic motion picture; a milestone in dinosaur annals that effectively jumpstarted a whole generation of creatures, beasts and nasties spawned from our seemingly never ending careless handling of atomic toys.

Intelligently directed, reasonably acted and, in the hands of Ray Harryhausen, a welcome return to a dinosaur that actually looked like a dinosaur rather than a pet shop lizard or a man in a suit. If THE BEAST FROM 20,000 FATHOMS was a poker hand, you'd be holding all aces.

The original model of "The Beast" (photo copyright © 1953 Warner Brothers)

"The idea was fresh at the time," recalls Freiberger, "but it had been done before. For whatever reason, the film brought back something that just ticked in people. I know it ticked in certain segments of the film community. I've been told that the producers of the remake of THE THING kept running BEAST over and over for inspiration."

THE BEAST FROM 20,000 FATHOMS begins in the Arctic where explorers, in a blinding snowstorm, spot the horrifying (and visually top notch) vision of something monstrous outlined against the snow. Before you can say Rhedosaurus, the creature, after some preliminary encounters with humans (and a great dinosaur vs lighthouse sequence) comes up

against the explorers and an aging paleontologist who, despite the scoffs of more enlightened masses, track the beast to its underwater lair.

The paleontologist in a diving bell becomes dinosaur chow and the Rhedosaurus, following some sort of ancient spawning instinct, makes its way to New York where the combination of its fierce nature,

(Photo copyright © 1953 Warner Brothers)

an unknown prehistoric disease and radioactivity germinating inside its body, soon has the Big Apple in shambles. Highlights of this dinosaur stomp include a cop being eaten, cars being flattened and the military's continued inability to put a dent in anything prehistoric.

The beast ends up at Coney Island, where our hero scientist and a military sharp shooter (played in cameo by a very young Lee Van Cleef), in a breathtaking encounter on the rollercoaster, kill the monster by shooting an atomic isotope into it.

The film, the first big dinosaur-directed effort of Eugene Lourie from a final shooting script by Fred Freiberger and Louis Morheim, starred Paul Christian, Paula Raymond, Cecil Kellaway, Kenneth Tobay and King Donovan.

Ray Harryhausen, fresh off the movie MIGHTY JOE YOUNG, remembers being called into the BEAST project by producers Hal Chester and Jack Dietz, who had been inspired, in large part, by the 1952 reissue success of KING KONG.

"They had an outline, written by Jack Dietz, for a film called IT CAME FROM BENEATH THE SEA. I felt I could contribute something to the film and so I accepted their offer."

In short order, IT CAME FROM BENEATH THE SEA became THE BEAST FROM 20,000 FATHOMS, Eugene Lourie was hired to direct and Freiberger and Morheim were given their marching orders.

"Hal Chester told us, 'We have a dinosaur, we want it resurrected in the Arctic, now come up with a storyline,'" says Freiberger. "So Lou and I went away and started writing. That first draft came real fast, in something like a month. Of course there were the rewrites."

And at least one "violent but friendly" argument between Freiberger and producer Chester, centering around when the audience should see the monster.

"I felt we should hold back the beast," relates Freiberger, "and not show it so soon. But Hal said 'You don't understand. I've spent a fortune on this thing and if you think I'm going to hold it back and only show it for two minutes, you're out of your mind.' Well, it was Hal's film and so that's why the creature shows up about a half hour earlier in the film than I would have liked. Holding it back and playing up the suspense is the way I would have gone with it."

Harryhausen recalls that while the script was being written, Chester decided to bring one other influential hand into the mix. "The producer came in one day with a copy of THE SATURDAY EVENING POST that contained Ray Bradbury's short story, 'The Foghorn.' The story had an illustration of a dinosaur attacking a lighthouse. He said to the writers and myself, 'Look at this illustration and give me something like that.' So a scene was added that involved the creature and a lighthouse."

In the meantime, Harryhausen and Lourie were in deep discussion as to what kind of dinosaur their BEAST FROM 20,000 FATHOMS should be. And the consensus was that it should not be a known species.

"Since it was an atomic bomb based story, we wanted to use a creature of unknown origin," details Harryhausen. "We went through several changes and crossed several different kinds of animals. We came up with an initial design that was not quite what anybody wanted, so we went back to the drawing board and changed quite a bit of it. Finally we came up with what we later called a Rhedosaurus. Our dinosaur had the head of an Allosaurus, the body of a dragon, the fins of some kind of mythological creature and it walked on four legs*. What we came up with was nothing like any known dinosaur, but we felt it would do the picture much more justice if we had an animal that people had not seen before."

The FX man remembers that the film afforded him very little time for pre-production. Coming off MIGHTY JOE YOUNG and the luxury of a 47-man crew and Willis O'Brien's glass painting animation backdrop, did not prepare Harryhausen for the spartan working conditions that this $200,000 wonder required.

"The biggest challenge on BEAST was to come up with an inexpensive way to put the animal in present day scenery like the New

"The Beast From 20,000 Fathoms" eats the cyclone at Coney Island (photo copyright © 1953 Warner Brothers.)

York streets without building a lot of miniature sets and glass paintings for the background scenery," says Harryhausen. "So I thought about it for a while and came up with a process that we later called Dynamation."

The Dynamation process, as explained by Harryhausen, had the Rhedosaurus model animated, a frame at a time, against a blank process scene with a section of each frame covered with masking tape. The creature footage was then rear-projected behind live action footage and rephotographed. The film was then rewound, the masked off areas exposed and the scene rephotographed to include the foreground live action in the exposed portion of the frame.

"Basically, it is a process in which the animated dinosaur model is sandwiched in between the background and the foreground of the actual film," he explains. "The process was used extensively in the scenes in which the creature is destroying New York and the lighthouse attack sequence."

Harryhausen recalls "shooting quite a bit of dinosaur footage" in the six months prior to the start of the live action portion of the film. "Every scene was a challenge. It was the first thing I did on my own and I did not have a crew to back me up. Because of the limited budget, we had to make a lot of compromises. Fortunately, Eugene came from an art director's background and was very sympathetic to the idea of matching the animation and live action as closely as possible."

THE BEAST FROM 20,000 FATHOMS opened in June 1953. Critically and otherwise the film was a major success. Everybody loved it. Well....almost everybody.

Ray Bradbury complained long and loud that THE BEAST FROM 20,000 FATHOMS was a not too discreet steal of his "The Foghorn", and threatened to sue. His fury surrounding the notion of theft subsided, but has never really gone away. In response to a letter early in 1991, Bradbury once again recounted the slight.

"I had nothing to do with BEAST. They [the producers] plagiarized my story. I caught them at it and they paid up! Then they used my name to help them sell the film that, essentially, was not mine."

THE BEAST FROM 20,000 FATHOMS' reputation has grown as more and more historians have taken a second look at the film. But Harryhausen, in hindsight, stops short of calling the movie a classic.

"Whether or not it's a classic is up to the viewer," he states. "If the people love it, that's wonderful. We were telling the story of a prehistoric creature that was aroused by the atomic bomb. We took the time to explain things and give more to the project than anybody expected. I think for the time and the budget we did a creditable job."

The list of creatures that followed in THE BEAST FROM 20,000 FATHOMS' wake is endless. It is a cycle that shows no sign of waning; a cycle given its official blessing the day an atomic bomb blast woke a Rhedosaurus from a Mesozoic sleep and sent it scampering off into a blinding snowstorm.

7

"You call your Attorneyosaurus and I'll call mine"

With the roar of GODZILLA and THE BEAST FROM 20,000 FATHOMS ringing in the ears of filmmakers, dinosaur movies segued into the decade of peace and love seemingly primed to soar like a Pterodactyl. But best laid plans fall prey to low budgets and lazy filmmakers, resulting in dinosaur flicks in the first half of the '60s which were conspicuous by their mediocrity.

Thanks for this are owed, in no small measure, to the efforts of a campy little ditty called DINOSAURUS! (1960). The film, produced by the notorious "B" film honcho Jack H. Harris, comes upon a construction crew dredging a harbor on an isolated tropical island. The operation hooks something big in its dredge and is shocked to discover a Tyrannosaurus Rex, Brontosaurus and a cave

man lying frozen at the bottom of the ocean. The creatures are brought to shore where an errant lightning bolt brings them back to life.

Things get downright predictable as the Tyrannosaurus attacks the locals, the Brontosaurus eats plants, and the caveman, in some forced but somewhat funny moments, discovers the horror of modern day appliances. The caveman

6259-61

T-Rex takes on a crane in "Dinosaurus!" (photo© 1960 Universal International)

45

Bronto and puppet in "Dinosaurus!" (photo © 1960 Universal International)

eventually makes friends with a small island boy and they in turn make friends with and ride the Brontosaurus.

The film climaxes with the T-Rex attacking and killing the Brontosaurus, the prehistoric man dying in a cave-in and the leader of the construction crew, astride a steam shovel, fighting the surviving monster on the edge of a cliff. A sucker punch sends the last surviving relic off the cliff and screaming into the

end credits as the film's hero and heroine embrace. Yuck!

DINOSAURUS!, directed by Irwin S. Yeaworth Jr. from a Jean Yeaworth and Dan Weisburd script, and starring Ward Ramsey, Paul Lukather, Kristina Hanson and Alan Roberts, is essentially a children's film and, as such, has received an overly generous share of mixed reviews. Some tomes cite the film's unintentional humor and shoddiness of script and acting as a

strange kind of attraction. But the realists in the bunch are quick to point out that the emperor, in this case DINOSAURUS!, indeed has no clothes.

The primary culprits are the title creatures. The dinosaurs are rather bland looking creations from the usually very good KONG alum Marcel Delgado. The animation is slow, clumsy and totally unconvincing work by Tim Baar, Wah Chang and Gene Warren. Nice try, guys.

Dinosaurs went 0 for 2 that year when Irwin Allen unleashed a glossy but very condescending knock-off remake of THE LOST WORLD.

Hope sprang eternal when it was announced that Allen's trip to the lost plateau would have Willis O'Brien on board as technical advisor. Hope fell on its butt when O'Brien suggested stop motion animation as the way to bring the dinosaurs to life, and Allen said thanks but no thanks. But Allen remained confident that he would do the right thing.

Advance hype on this Allen directed, Allen-Charles Bennett scripted film rang out with the claim that "These dinosaurs will be the most lifelike ever filmed." Print ads for the film featured dinosaur looking dinosaurs and led audiences to believe that this LOST WORLD would match the magic of the 1925 original.

So you can imagine the shock and disappointment when the film opened and audiences discovered that Allen wasted the talents of

There goes London Bridge courtesy of "Gorgo" (photo © 1961 MGM)

47

Irwin Allen's disastrous remake of "The Lost World." Nice lizard, huh? (photo © 1960 20th Century Fox.)

Claude Rains, Michael Rennie, Fernando Lamas, Jill St. John and David Hedison on a cut-rate adventure that features lizards and alligators with fins and horns glued on. The film looked reasonably well and played close to Doyle's story (although the entire dinosaur on the loose in London sequence was jettisoned), but there's a stink of disrespect for the genre permeating THE LOST WORLD that has only gotten worse with age. A real black moment.

VALLEY OF THE DRAGONS (1961), based on a Jules Verne novel about two men swept in a windstorm onto a prehistoric comet, was the latest film to dredge up the giant lizard footage from ONE MILLION B.C. The film, starring Cesare Danova and Sean McClory, was a minor effort whose dinosaurs played second fiddle to the assets of Joan Stanley (PLAYBOY's Miss November 1958), who played a stone age Eve.

Be afraid, be very afraid of this loser, "Reptilicus".

GORGO (1961) was a major step up from previous '60s efforts and little wonder. Director Eugene Lourie had a lot of experience in prehistoric matters, having helmed THE BEAST FROM 20,000 FATHOMS and THE GIANT BEHEMOTH. GORGO, written by John Loring and Daniel Hyatt, is basically BEAST and BEHEMOTH done man-in-a-suit style.

Producers Frank Maurice and Hyman King had the bright idea to unleash yet another prehistoric monster on another big city (London) and approached Lourie to direct. The director, having been to this well twice before, was reluctant. But Lourie, in a FANTASTIC FILMS interview, recalled what changed his mind.

"My daughter cried at the end of BEAST FROM 20,000 FATHOMS when the creature died. I knew that, to please her, that someday I would have to write a story where the creature wins and just goes away. When GORGO was offered to me, I saw my chance."

GORGO, starring William Travers and William Sylvester, opens off the coast of Ireland as a pair of fly-by-the-seat-of-their-pants salvagers discover a prehistoric monster terrorizing fishermen on a small island. The duo, following a claustrophobic encounter in a diving bell, capture the creature ship it off to London where, despite pleas for scientific sanity from the paleontological community, it becomes a sideshow attraction at a circus.

The scientist's warning that the captured monster is a juvenile and that any angry parent might be lurking in the mists, becomes reality when momma Gorgo swims ashore and stomps on London Bridge, Big Ben, a number of other landmarks and an ineffectual British army before freeing its offspring and disappearing back into the sea.

GORGO is a fairly effective, no frills effort. The combination of the man in the suit (actually four men in a suit, according to credits), miniatures and live action scenes is comparable to similar work in the original GODZILLA. Lourie's direction is energetic and the acting is workmanlike. Bottom line: Unpretentious filmmaking can add life to even the most shopworn of tales.

So how bad is bad? Bad enough for American International Pictures to sue? Well, REPTILICUS (1962) is that bad.

But more on that later. Suffice it to say that REPTILICUS is the classic example of a pretty good idea done in by a bad case of the bad that starts with bad directing, acting and special effects, and works its way down to that most unpardonable of sins: a dopey looking dinosaur.

The film, directed by Sid Pink and written by Ib Melchior, opens with promise as oil drillers off the coast of Denmark feel a sudden jolt as their drill bit bites into something hard. That something turns out to be the well-preserved tail

section of a dinosaur. Scientists are immediately trotted out and proclaim they have developed a new process that can regenerate tissue and (are you ready for this?) grow an entire specimen out of that section.

Now as preposterous as all this may sound, the movie, to this point, almost works. Sure the badly dubbed, stilted English, mouthed by cardboard actors Carl Ottoson, Ann Smyrner and Asbjorn Andersen, is hilarious. But the plot is so "out there" that you're literally on the edge of your seat waiting for the inevitable to happen— which is when a bad guy deliberately speeds up the growth process and a full blown dinosaur escapes the lab and takes a trip into downtown Copenhagen.

Alas, the dinosaur appears at this point and we are treated to a just plain stupid looking marionette hopping around on visible wires. The monster lurches after badly edited scenes of supposedly terrified crowds running (and laughing) down city streets. It spits out putrid green slime and basically wastes a whole lot of valuable film stock. At one moment in the film, Denmark's feeble military attacks and succeeds in knocking off an arm. Now this puppet is really mad! More lurching and bad dialogue ensues before science and a nuclear knockout device administers a fatal blow and the creature is hauled off and burned.

The end? Far from it. For at the

fade we see the aforementioned blown off appendage floating to the bottom of the see, where it begins to regenerate.

Oh no! Not REPTILICUS II!

"Sid had the idea about a big reptile that destroys a city," recalls Melchior. "He also had the contacts in Denmark. So he asked me to come up with a script and set it in that location."

Melchior claims that, although he worked with Pink on a number of projects, he is, presently, "not a big Sid Pink fan." And one of the main reasons for that centers around REPTILICUS.

"Pink took my script and did some things to it that I was not happy with. He wrote in the scenes where the monster spits out that green slime which was ridiculous. He also insisted on using Danish, Swedish and German actors who spoke English with heavy accents. He told them to speak very distinctly and slowly so that you could read their lips. But because he directed the actors that way, we ended up having to have the entire film redubbed after it was completed."

Melchior's shots at REPTILICUS were not just isolated gripes. When the folks at AIP (who co-financed the picture) screened the finished product, which was awash in bad special effects, poor editing and mismatched shots, they were so incensed that they filed a lawsuit against producer Pink.

Pink was not really in a position to fight the suit (let alone win it, according to those few who saw the answer print and were not immediately turned to stone), so he threw up his hands and passed the baton to Melchior.

"AIP said the film was unreleasable so they asked me to fix it," relates the writer/director. "I shot some additional scenes in the states and re-edited portions of the film."

AIP still hated it, but felt REPTILICUS was now marginally releasable and dropped the lawsuit. One of the cuts made for the U.S. version of the film is a sequence in which Reptilicus flys. If you're a real glutton for punishment, the European version containing that scene is out there somewhere. But if you've already seen the U.S. version, you're probably not that brave.

Dinosaurs and related kin also made appearances in JOURNEY TO THE BEGINNING OF TIME (1967), in which young boys on a raft drift backwards on the River of Time and discover some serviceable dinosaurs and mammoths. In one element of that classic exercise in time travel confusion, JOURNEY TO THE CENTER OF TIME (1967), Anthony Eisley and Scott Brady fend off stock footage that's older than dirt. A dinosaur scene in the script for the much better THE TIME TRAVELLERS (1964) was never filmed because of budget problems.

The '60s were definitely shaping up as a decade to forget. But don't jump ship, for Ray Harryhausen was about to step in and save the purist's bacon with a powerful one-two punch: ONE MILLION YEARS B.C. and THE VALLEY OF GWANGI.

"Gorgo" (photo © 1961 MGM)

8

The Valley of B.C.

Ray Harryhausen went on to complete quite a hit list after cutting his teeth on THE BEAST FROM 20,000 FATHOMS. But the critical raves accorded the special effects legend on such efforts as THE 7TH VOYAGE OF SINBAD and JASON AND THE ARGONAUTS, could never really separate Harryhausen, at least in thought, from his true love.

"I've always had a love for dinosaurs," he says. "I started out with the dinosaur genre and although I've gone on to do other things, I was always on the lookout for the opportunity to do a dinosaur movie again."

Harryhausen's passion had been teased a number of times throughout the early '60s when

A prehistoric turtle, courtesy Ray Harryhausen in "One Million Years B.C."

T-Rex terrorizes Raquel Welch in "One Million Years B.C."

Hammer Films, in hot pursuit of the rights to remake KING KONG, had contacted him about bringing his animation expertise to the project.

"I was interested," says Harryhausen. "But I always felt that KONG was a classic and, unless you remade the same picture in color, you could not do any better."

Hammer never got the KING KONG rights, but they did manage to secure the rights to remake ONE MILLION B.C. Once again, a call was placed to Harryhausen.

"I definitely saw the possibilities in a remake of ONE MILLION B.C.," he recalls. "The original used lizards blown up on a projection screen. I felt I could do much better with animation, so I accepted the challenge."

The remake, entitled ONE MILLION YEARS B.C. (1966), essentially fit Harryhausen's theory on redoing KING KONG. It is the same story as the 1940 film and it was proposed to be shot in color. The film, directed by Don Chaffey and starring Raquel Welch, John Richardson and Martine Beswicke, was written by the movie's producer, Michael Carreras, who, in a FANGORIA interview with Steve

Swires, jokingly claimed, "I may be the only member of the Writer's Guild who continues to get royalty checks for a script containing no dialogue."

An homage to the original ONE MILLION B.C. and its low budget roots appears in the remake with token appearances by a giant Iguana and a big spider. But the Brontosaurus, Allosaurus, Triceratops, Pterodactyl and giant turtle that provide the lion's share of the film's creature action are Harryhausen's animation work and it is a job he took very seriously.

"I felt the dinosaurs should be as accurate as possible, because so many people, having attended museums, were so aware of what a dinosaur should look like. So I went to the London Natural History Museum, studied the skeletons and took a number of photographs. I also recruited a member of the museum staff who was involved in dinosaur anatomy to help me create the models."

Harryhausen's creature models, with the exception of the Pterodactyl, were of equal proportion. The Pterodactyl was designed to a larger scale to make it functional in close-ups with larger models. The models were made of armature laden ball and socketed skeletons that allowed movement of individual appendages and tension to pull against the rubber skin put over the skeleton.

While the script for ONE MILLION YEARS B.C. went through all of the inevitable rewrites,

Harryhausen, ever the budget conscious filmmaker, was storyboarding the animation sequences and peppering the director with preproduction sketches designed to avoid the sin of shooting unnecessary footage. The FX man was also busy contributing to the subtle modernization of B.C.'s very old story.

"The script was based on Hal Roach's original story," he recalls, "but everybody was concerned that it have some modern touches. We were attempting to do something better; especially when it came to the dinosaur sequences.

"The Allosaurus raiding the village in the original film was a man in a suit, so they had to hide it behind a bush to make it look effective. With animation we felt we did not have those limitations and so we could elaborate and expand that sequence. The attitude was the same with the scene in which the Allosaurus fights the Triceratops (the equivalent of the giant lizard battle in the original). The big challenge was to make the scene as exciting as possible and yet stick to the basic principles that were used in the original movie."

The island of Lonzorotti in the Canary Islands, a terribly prehistoric and volcanic looking place, was chosen as the location for the film. Harryhausen and director Chaffey (who he had previously worked with on JASON AND THE ARGONAUTS) went into the project in synch as to what Hammer Films' biggest budgeted effort to date would require.

"Don was very familiar with what I needed and that was important, not only for me to lay out the live action animated sequences but, in many cases, to direct them myself so that six months later, when I was animating the dinosaurs in the studio, I would be able to put the whole scene together."

Actress Martine Beswicke, who plays the primitive rival of Welch's in the film, recalled, in a FANGORIA interview with Steve Swires, that on the set of ONE MILLION YEARS B.C. Harryhausen was the subject of awe.

"He was very quiet and deep and totally committed to what he was doing," said the actress. "He personally directed all the scenes involving special effects. For the dinosaur attacks, he rode in the back of a truck mounted with a camera and told the actors where to look and move. He needed our eye lines to work with and so he had us react to his hand as if it was the creature."

The on-going question during the film's making was not whether Chaffey and Harryhausen could pull off a respectable dinosaur outing, but rather both could survive the at-large reputation of Raquel Welch as temperamental and hard to get along with.

Producer Charles Schneer, a long-time Harryhausen associate who was privy to the behind the scenes battles, claimed in a Steve Swires conducted STARLOG interview, "When it comes to dinosaurs, everything else takes second place for Ray. Unfortunately [in ONE

Similar scenes from Ray Harryhausen in "The Valley of Gwangi" and "20 Million Miles to Earth".

57

MILLION YEARS B.C.] he came up against somebody who told him, 'This isn't your picture, it's my picture.' Frankly, it wasn't a happy experience for Ray."

"Raquel drove me and everybody else crazy," remembered Beswicke. "But I had a great deal of compassion for her because her ass was on the line in that picture."

Harryhausen admits that he was very insistent that such scenes as Welch being carried aloft by the Pterodactyl and running from dinosaurs be precise. But he poo-poos the notion of an on-set war.

"She was very cooperative and very easy to work with," he reflects. "The rumor had gotten around that we had clashes on the set and it was not the truth. I believe what happened was that the joke going around at that time about who made the picture, Raquel Welch or my dinosaurs, got out of hand and into the press that Raquel and I were at each other's throats. That was not the case. She worked very hard and never complained."

ONE MILLION YEARS B.C.

finished on time, on budget and, although Harryhausen's Brontosaurus had its screen time ultimately cut to what he describes as "a walk through," he is basically happy with the results.

"Some people said it was the best dinosaur movie ever made. Personally, I think the definitive dinosaur movie has yet to be made. But I was quite happy with the results."

Harryhausen's dinosaur fix lasted less than two years before the need to bring prehistoric monsters back to life struck again. The urge

A storyboard from "Valley of Gwangi" (photo copyright © 1969 Warner Brothers)

also led him to reteam with long-time producer Charles Schneer. Looking for a project, the pair went straight to the garage of Harryhausen's then California home where a pair of Willis O'Brien relics lay waiting for regeneration: the skimpy storyline of WAR EAGLES and the script for GWANGI. Harryhausen was quite familiar with the latter.

"I used to visit Willis at the studio when he and Marcel Delgado were working on the film. They had a model of an Allosaurus and all manner of glass paintings and story-boards laying around. I loved the idea of dinosaurs and cowboys. You could not ask for a better combination.

"I don't know why it did not happen. You'd have to ask RKO executives who are all underground. I guess you'll have to ask them in the next life," he laughs.

Schneer took a look at both projects. He recalled his reaction to both in a STARLOG interview with Steve Swires: "I turned down WAR EAGLES because I couldn't see how to get a script out of it. But I read the original GWANGI script and said, 'Let's do it.'"

Schneer and Harryhausen agreed that O'Brien's basic story needed some work, beginning with

---

(At left) Ray Harryhausen and actor Richard Carlson tame a prehistoric beast in "The Valley of Gwangi" (photo © 1969 Warner Brothers)

---

the more marketable title THE VALLEY OF GWANGI. Screenwriter William E. Bast, with dialogue contributions from Julian Moore, fashioned the tale of a wild west circus in turn of the century Mexico whose owners discover an unbelievable exhibit in the guise of a prehistoric miniature horse Eohippus.

The creature escapes and, with a bunch of cowboys in pursuit, returns to its home; a secluded valley inhabited by a variety of live dinosaurs. After witnessing the monsters do battle, our reckless cowpokes decide that an Allosaurus in hand is worth an Eohippus in the bush and, in a spectacular series of sequences, run down the carnivorous dinosaur on horseback, rope it, tie it down and transport it to a bullring where it is put on display. In due course, the dinosaur escapes, fights an elephant and ends up in a church where it dies in a fire.

Schneer had a long and mutually rewarding relationship with Columbia Pictures and so it seemed a lock that GWANGI would ultimately fly the Columbia banner. But Harryhausen remembers that it was not meant to be.

"Columbia did not want to invest the money and I also think the story did not really appeal to them. The bottom line was that we had to look for other financing. But we got lucky when Ken Hyman, who had helped finance ONE MILLION YEARS B.C., bought Warner Bros. When Charles took the script and my sketches to Ken, he liked the story and we made a deal."

With the story and special effects storyboarded to the nth degree, producer Schneer felt he could risk handing over the directorial reigns to relative unknown James O'Connolly. "Since the picture was already pre-designed, I figured he could not go too far wrong," said Schneer.

Schneer also couldn't go too far wrong with the cast, which included such stalwart second rung stars as James Franciscus, Richard Carlson and relative newcomer Gila Golan.

THE VALLEY OF GWANGI commenced filming in 1967 in Almira Spain. Harryhausen, as in previous films, had a major hand in directing the live action elements of the stop motion that would be added later. And the film, he recalls, required a diversity of styles.

"The scene in which the Allosaurus fights the elephant was done in a sandwiching process that was similar to the process we used in BEAST FROM 20,000 FATHOMS," he says. "The Eohippus model had to be animated differently because, despite its size, it was a horse and to make it ring true, it had to walk like a horse.

"The sequence where the cowboys chase the Allosaurus and rope it, were easily the most difficult in the film. I had to make animated ropes with real ropes, stop motion animation of the cowboys and horses with the live action, and it all had to be done in quick cuts. It was very difficult and complex."

GWANGI was also not the smooth precision ride that the previous Schneer-Harryhausen collaborations had been. Bumps in the road centered around the emotional stamina of the director and the vocal abilities of one of the actors. In the case of director O'Connolly, Schneer related, "O'Connolly seemed to have lost interest in the middle of shooting. I don't think he enjoyed making the film and he just didn't have his heart in it when we were about halfway through."

Casting came back to haunt the film the first time actress Golan opened her mouth. Schneer had cast the Israeli actress in the role of an American cowgirl as a favor to Warner Bros, but he knew going in that her heavy accent would sabotage the proceedings.

"I had hoped we would not have to dub her," related the producer, "but once I listened to her delivery, I knew her voice would have to be redone."

As is the case with all of Harryhausen's work, GWANGI took nearly two years to complete. Unfortunately, in the meantime, the regime that had given its full support to the film had sold out to new management. And what usually happens when the new kid takes over happened to THE VALLEY OF GWANGI.

"The new management at Warner Bros. was not supportive of GWANGI at all," laments Harryhausen. "They did not know how to market it. They dumped it out there with very little publicity.

Because so little was done for the film, people thought that the title meant it was a dubbed Japanese monster movie and did not go see it. The film was given a 'G' rating, which also turned off a large segment of the audience that would go to a movie like this."

Consequently, THE VALLEY OF GWANGI came and went in 1969 with nary a whimper of recognition. Although the film, on the strength of Harryhausen's truly excellent creations, has gained some critical stature over the years, both Schneer and Harryhausen agree that "GWANGI is not one of our best."

Ray Harryhausen would go on to make more successful movies that included THE GOLDEN VOYAGE OF SINBAD, SINBAD AND THE EYE OF THE TIGER and the often maligned (but truly representative of Harryhausen's skills) CLASH OF THE TITANS. Harryhausen retired shortly after TITANS.

"There reaches a point where you can't see yourself spending another year of your life in a darkened room twisting little models around. But I still love the work and I miss it sometimes."

And that longing, in contemplating further adventures in dinosaur filmmaking, results in at least one mention on his personal wish list. "If the opportunity arose, I would love to do THE LOST WORLD over again in a different way."

Does that mean Harryhausen's retirement is not quite so permanent?

"Well," he says, a gleam in his eye, "you never say never."

9

Somebody Did See It

To make good dinosaur movies, or not to make good dinosaur movies? That was the question filmmakers asked themselves during the decade of the '70s. The answer? Sometimes they did and sometimes they didn't.

TROG (1970) answers both questions. Sort of. Joan Crawford's last film is really a bad missing link movie in which the title stone age creature stumbles into polite society, tears up a small town and ultimately gets his. It barely squeaks by as a passable dinosaur movie in the sequence where the Troglodyte in question takes a scientifically induced nap and dreams of his prehistoric past which turns out to be stock footage from Irwin Allen's THE ANIMAL WORLD.

On the up side, Hammer Films chose 1970 to capitalize on the success of ONE MILLION YEARS B.C. with another dinosaur adventure, WHEN DINOSAURS RULED THE EARTH. This tale of star-crossed stone age lovers from warring tribes (an almost direct plot theft from ONE MILLION YEARS B.C.) was based on a skeletal outline submitted by science fiction writer J. G. Ballard.

Hammer took the treatment and shipped it over to the island of Malta where their first choice to direct the film was vacationing following the rigors of directing the spy thriller ASSIGNMENT K.

"They brought me a very vague treatment," recalled director Val Guest in a STARLOG interview with Steve Swires. "I said yes, I would do it, and sat down to write the script. I had not seen ONE MILLION YEARS B.C. and so I had no preconceptions about [making] a dinosaur movie."

Guest found that casting this prehistoric story produced an anxious moment or two. He had no problem with casting Robin Hawdon, who had played a minor role in the Guest film THE DAY THE EARTH CAUGHT FIRE, as the male lead. But when Hammer Films head James Carreras offered up former PLAYBOY playmate Victoria Vetri for the pivotal female role, Guest remembered being "horrified."

"She was not a very good actress. She did not handle the technical effects very well and she just could not do very much. Fortunately, all I had to do was keep her moving and looking reasonably attractive."

As the title indicates, WHEN DINOSAURS RULED THE EARTH was up to its Pterodactyl in dinosaurs, courtesy of special effects supervisor, Jim Danforth. Danforth, in conference with producer Aida Young, was happy to

(Photo copyright © 1970 Warner Brothers)

A Triceratops in "When Dinosaurs Ruled the Earth" (photo copyright © 1970 Warner Brothers)

discover that Hammer, like its B.C. predecessor, wanted real-looking creatures.

David Allen, who assisted Danforth in the construction of a variety of dinosaurs, recalls that, effects-wise, the approach to making the model dinosaurs was all over the place.

"The main mother dinosaur was totally fabricated onto the metal armature frame; pretty much along the lines of how Marcel Delgado used to build things," he says. "The Chasmosaurus was cast, molded and sculpted except for the bony frill around the head which was built right into the skull. The baby dinosaur was also molded and sculpted.

"The animating of the dinosaurs were done basically the way Ray Harryhausen did in ONE MILLION YEARS B.C. Some matte paintings were used in a couple of scenes in conjunction with the Dynamation process, but it was basically the animation approach as envisioned by Harryhausen."

Allen claims that while WHEN DINOSAURS RULED THE EARTH contained "less animation than you would see in a normal Harryhausen picture," he was left with the impression that "artistically Jim was trying to move the work a little further than what Harryhausen did."

Director Guest seconded that

"The Land That Time Forgot" (photo copyright © A.I.P.)

notion when he said that every one of Danforth's creatures had a personality. "There is a scene where one of the cave people spears a Pterodactyl as it comes swooping in to attack a girl. When it was speared, Jim gave the Pterodactyl a wince so that you felt the creature had actually been hurt."

Guest maintained that, with Danforth on the set much of the time, shooting the live action por-

tion of the film was relatively easy. Using a very detailed storybook that outlined where effects would go and how the actors should react, Guest, with the aid of poles (to simulate the dinosaurs), lines in the sand and directions for actors on where to look, was able to draw the live action into a seamless counter to the creatures that would be added later.

A highlight during filming for

both cast and crew turned out to be the lensing of two nude scenes involving Vetri. Those scenes ultimately appeared in the European cut of the film, but were deleted for US audiences when Warner Bros. decided a "G" rated version of DINOSAURS was in their box office best interest.

But as filming progressed, it became evident that there was trouble in prehistoric paradise.

WHEN DINOSAURS RULED THE EARTH began to go over schedule—due primarily to Danforth's reportedly perfectionist nature when it came to the dinosaur effects.

"There was some bitterness at the time," relates Allen. "Things were taking longer than expected.

Jim was working to his own usual high standards and, as far as that film was concerned, it was going to take as long as it took. Finally, Hammer just gave up protesting and just hoped for the best."

Hammer's faith, to a certain extent, was rewarded, for while WHEN DINOSAURS RULED

THE EARTH did not have the kind of box office success of ONE MILLION YEARS B.C., the film was every bit the artistic success its predecessor was.

In the mid '70s, writer David Gerrold came up with a dandy time travel, dinosaur-hunting script called DEATH BEAST. The

"The People That Time Forgot" (photo © A.I.P.)

"The Last Dinosaur"

filmmakers liked it. Their check to Gerrold cleared. Everybody was happier than a pigasaurus in poop. But the honeymoon ended three weeks before production was set to start.

"The director said he wanted me to add a scene where this ferocious dinosaur tiptoes up behind a girl and surprises her," Gerrold remembers with a laugh. "I said, 'Do you know what it sounds like when a dinosaur tiptoes?' I told them it was a stupid gag and that the audience was going to laugh at it. I refused to write it. The next thing I knew, they cancelled the whole deal. I wrote them a check on the spot and they gave me back the rights to the script. I subsequently wrote a novel based on the script. And the book came out a lot better than I'm convinced the movie would have."

Dinosaurs did not resurface again until the mid-1970's and when they did, it was with a resounding thud thanks to a trio of

David Allen creates the "Crater Lake Monster" (photo copyright © Crown International)

Edgar Rice Burroughs' "At the Earth's Core" (photo © A.I.P.)

bargain basement Edgar Rice Burroughs abominations: THE LAND THAT TIME FORGOT (1975), AT THE EARTH'S CORE (1976) and THE PEOPLE THAT TIME FORGOT (1977). All three features, released by Amicus/AIP and directed by Kevin Connor, star actor Doug McClure and some of the worst dinosaur effects ever committed to celluloid. You name it. Men in monster suits, dinosaur heads held aloft on poles, flying reptiles on visible wires. If it's cheesy, it's in these films.

All three of these childish outings are fairly straightforward interpretations of Burroughs' adventures in Caprona and Pellucidar, but the cheap-jack nature of the dinosaurs totally destroys the potential for anything other than laughs. One could forgive an actor for stumbling into a mess like this once. But for McClure to willingly go on and do two more, knowing full well they would not get any better?

Why, Doug?

"Quite honestly, I wasn't as well off as I would like to have been," said McClure during a surprisingly candid interview. "When you're going through a divorce and have children to support, it becomes hard to say no to certain things."

A little higher up on the evolutionary scale—but not much—was the 1977 movie for television, THE LAST DINOSAUR. This made in Japan adventure, which stars Richard Boone and Joan Van Ark, tells the story of the consummate hunter who, with the aid of a burrowing device called the Thrust Polar Boarer, arrives at a lost world....the better to capture the ultimate prey, the last surviving Tyrannosaurus Rex. The film gives it the old college try and anything with Richard Boone in it is worth a look, but all the camera tricks in the world can't disguise the fact that our T-Rex is an off-the-rack suit. Kids could do worse. Adults could definitely do better.

The prospect of WHEN DINO-SAURS RULED THE EARTH alum David Allen doing the stop motion animation work on THE CRATER LAKE MONSTER (1977), held out hope that dinosaur films in the 70's might make a rebound. What the film turned out to be was a rim shot.

This William Stromberg directed quickie opens with a meteor crashing into a mountain lake and bringing a long dormant Plesiosaur back to life that terrorizes the locals before meeting its maker in a battle to the death with a snow plow. The acting is bad. The story is predictable. But the dinosaur sequences make this film worth a look.

"I don't remember thinking too much about the script one way or the other," remembers Allen. "All I knew was that here was my chance to key my first film and so I went for it."

Allen's instructions were to create some kind of sea serpent-like creatures. This he accomplished by sculpting a head, neck and body onto a metal armature. A big, full-sized head was created for close-ups. For the animation process, Allen reached back into an old bag of tricks.

"Because I had worked on WHEN DINOSAURS RULED THE EARTH, I had some practical experience with the Dynamation process, so that's what I used on this film. The sea serpent sequences were all done on the original dupe negative rather than putting the whole thing through the normal optical process. THE CRATER LAKE MONSTER was not going to be a film to enlarge the vocabulary of special effects," he laughs.

THE CRATER LAKE MON-STER, by Allen's estimation, contained less than three minutes of actual stop motion footage. Most of that centered on the final dinosaur vs snow plow scenes, but small snippets of the creature chasing a car, threatening a boat and some random attack shots also stand out.

"What's there is good," contends Allen, "but the main problem with the film is a shortage of FX shots of the creature."

A shortage made all the more maddening by the fact that additional dinosaur-laden sequences were actually lost or thrown away in the editing room, according to Allen.

"Jim Danforth helped me on that film and he did this real nice scene in which the shadow of the snow plow blade crosses the creature's back. It was only a couple of feet of film and, as near as I can figure, it was just tossed out without anybody giving it a second thought.

"There was also the scene at the very end when the dinosaur crawls into the frame and slowly expires. When the camera shooting the scene was backwound, it wasn't turned all the way back and so we ended up losing the first five feet of the shot. So all you see in the finished film is the creature just laying there."

Crown International picked up the film for distribution and then, amazingly, promoted the film with a totally deceptive poster that depicted the Allosaurus roaming around a forest. The poster did not help or hinder the film, which died a quick death in theatres.

Allen's assessment of THE CRATER LAKE MONSTER falls laughingly into cliche: "My feeling is what everybody says when they come out of a screening room. For what it is, it's not a bad little movie."

Another film saved by stop motion appeared in 1978 in the guise of a low budget independent called PLANET OF THE DINO-SAURS. The film, directed by James Shea from a Ralph Lucas script, is essentially KING DINO-SAUR minus the bomb.

Astronauts land on a planet, are menaced by all manner of prehistoric animals, fight them and finally set up shop in this Garden of Eden. The acting, featuring James Whitworth of THE HILLS

HAVE EYES and a bunch of unknowns, is passable. The storyline is fairly mediocre. But what makes this film aces is the very good stop motion dinosaurs (courtesy of Stephen Czerkas, James Aupperle and Doug Beswick) that roam these low budget plains. This is not Harryhausen quality animation, but it's pretty damned close.

PLANET OF THE DINOSAURS suffered a GWANGI-like fate but has been known to show up on the tube from time to time. Worth marking your TV GUIDE for.

Worth going out of your way to avoid in 1979 were a pair of JAWS-inspired films that substituted prehistoric animals for sharks. The first, UP FROM THE DEPTHS, featured a prehistoric fish turning island swimmers into the blue plate special. The Philippines lensed feature toplined Sam Bottoms and was directed by Roger Corman's main man, Charles B. Griffith.

MONSTER (a.k.a. MONSTEROID), filmed in South America and California, finds a land and sea creature harassing local villagers and an American construction crew. It's watchable only for the strange gathering of actors who were talked (or blackmailed) into appearing. The cast includes Anthony Eisley, John Carradine, Cesar Romero and Jim Mitchum.

"There was really no way to do this film right," recalled Eisley in a FANGORIA interview with Tom Weaver. "We felt that we would go in, get a few bucks out of it and nobody would ever see the film. The only flaw in that theory was that somebody did see it."

10

Right Project Wrong Time

Filmmakers had seemingly gotten hip to the dinosaur movie game by the time the decade of the 80's rolled around. Technology had long since evolved to the point where nobody was going to be caught dead blowing up a monitor lizard and passing it off as a Dimetrodon.

A man in a rubber suit? Well, maybe. But a giant lizard? A pox on the thought!

But while the ability was definitely there, nothing really jumped out of the 80's and bit hard like Harryhausen's work did in the '60s. In fact, the most exciting news off the dinosaur teletype in this decade were two projects that appeared headed for the dinosaur hall of fame but, through circumstances that will be discussed in a moment, never got out of the blocks.

Not only did CAVEMAN (1981) get out of the blocks, but it actually finished the race as a modest box office success. The first "deliberate" prehistoric comedy, starring Ringo Starr, Barbara Bach and early appearances by budding stars Dennis Quaid and Shelley Long, tells the slapstick story of an outcast from a prehistoric tribe who forms his own tribe which consists of equally bumbling cave blokes.

The comedy in this Carl Gottlieb-directed film you can take or leave (some moments are actually quite funny), but the appearance of a stop motion T-Rex, a horned lizard, a wolf lizard and a Pterodactyl, done up comic style by

Ringo Starr and Barbara Bach in "Caveman" (photo © United Artists)

13562

Jim Danforth and David Allen, makes the trip back in time worthwhile. They and the effects team set about creating dinosaurs that fit the film's comic sensibility.

"Because it was a comedy, it definitely dictated how we sculpted the dinosaurs," recounts Allen. "We sculpted them in a quasi real style that exaggerated certain facial features while keeping the creatures basically realistic looking. We used the Dynamation animation process and used VistaVision backgrounds which, I've been told, helped enhance the quality of the stop motion effects."

It took nearly 50 years for filmmakers to attempt a second movie about the Loch Ness Monster. Sad to say, THE LOCH NESS HORROR (1982) trys to be a number of things and fails miserably at all of them. One moment of this hack business has the title Plesiosaur (which looks passable in the water, but like a Macy's parade balloon when it attacks on land) acting like Jaws. The next, we're thrown headfirst into a half-assed mystery involving a Nazi plane at the bottom of the loch. Throw in poachers finding a Nessie egg and the worst Scottish accents in the history of film, and you have a movie that's so bad it's bad.

Lisa Henson, in 1983, got the bright idea to do a dinosaur movie. It helped her cause that she was an executive at Warner Bros., and it certainly did not hurt that her father, Jim Henson, had the skills to make the project a reality.

Henson, armed with a stack of dinosaur books, went to the Virgin Islands where her father was vacationing, the better to convince him to make a dinosaur movie his third non-Muppet film. Production designer/artist Bill Stout was not in the picture at this point. But, thanks to an unlikely ally, he would shortly be smack dab in the middle of it.

"Jim was going over the books when his cook came by and said, 'Those books are nothing. I've got a dinosaur book that will knock your socks off,'" remembers Stout. "He showed Jim and Lisa my book of dinosaur paintings and they noticed my film background. Jim told his daughter to look me up when she got back and to see if I were interested in doing a movie."

Stout was and subsequently wrote the screenplay, contributing nine months worth of design work on the DARK CRYSTAL-style dinosaur fantasy film.

The script, which had the working title of NATURAL HISTORY PROJECT, was a coming of age tale of a young duckbilled Corythosaurus (Cory) who, through a series of adventures and close encounters with the dreaded T-Rex, grows to dinosaur adulthood with the aid of dinosaur buddies Mr. Sauroloff, Strack, Ms. Alamo and Pterry. During Cory's odyssey, he witnesses his mother's disappearance during a Corythosaurus stampede, challenges a huge Triceratops, is caught in a fierce sandstorm and ultimately finds true love as only a dinosaur can.

"We called it THE NATURAL HISTORY PROJECT because we were afraid somebody else would pick up on the idea before we could get it developed," says Stout. "I created a nice variety of dinosaurs on that film. The way Jim and I were planning to shoot the dinosaurs was with a combination of stop motion animation and puppetry."

Unfortunately, Henson's idea and Stout's script was very similar to the animated dinosaur film which was being developed across town at Amblin by Steven Spielberg and Don Bluth.

"When Warner Bros. found that out they cancelled the project," moans Stout. "The reason was that they did not want it to look like they were copying Spielberg."

Stout did not have time to curse the fates for later that same year he was contacted by director Steve Miner, who had the bright idea of making a U.S. version of GODZILLA. The Fred Dekker penned script, entitled GODZILLA: KING OF THE MONSTERS, borrowed, coincidentally, elements of the never-produced VOLCANO MONSTERS and, somewhat intentionally, from GORGO.

In a nutshell, this updated tale would have centered on Godzilla who, in pursuit of its missing young, surfaces in San Francisco and destroys the city. The story would focus on a particular group of city dwellers as they attempt to survive the dinosaur onslaught.

Miner, who was partnered with Toho on the proposed project, had a specific goal in mind.

Godzilla: 1985 (Photo © 1985 Toho Films)

"I wanted to redo Godzilla with the attitude that the first one had never been made," he explains. "Godzilla in Japanese means half gorilla and half something else. What I felt was that in order to do Godzilla right, it had to be a dinosaur. And we knew going in that we were not going to make Godzilla a good monster. Our Godzilla was going to be very bad. He was going to come out of San Francisco Bay at night and really kill people."

Stout, who was hired to storyboard the proposed film, recalls that everyone was in agreement as to exactly what this new Godzilla should and should not be.

"Our goal was, instead of remaking a classic and automatically pissing off the people who loved the original, to take a good idea that we felt had not been executed very well and to do the film state of the art, Spielberg style using stop motion animation and puppetry."

The idea caught on big in the special effects community. Rick Baker leaped at the chance to make a cable-controlled Godzilla head. David Allen agreed to do the stop motion. Miner originally intended his vision of Godzilla to be lensed in 3-D, but the inherent difficulties of shooting stop motion, which is basically a 2-D process, caused Miner to abandon that element.

Miner began taking meetings with the likes of Warner Bros and other major studios; meetings with the likes of producers Jon Peters and Keith Barish. He would make surprising headway. Up to a point.

"I wasn't a real bankable director, which hurt the film's chances. The estimated budget to do the film right, $25-30 million, was considered too expensive. And the marketing people were convinced that no matter what our approach to making the film was, Godzilla would still be a kid's movie and would have a limited audience."

"The response during those pitch meetings was the same all up and down the line," says Stout. "They would say, 'This is fantastic, this is great.' Then he would get to the guy at the top who had the final yes or no decision and it would always be no. A lot of big budget films had been released at that time and bombed and so no studio wanted to risk the money it would take to do the movie right. I'm convinced that if Steve had gone to them a few years earlier or later, it might have happened. Unfortunately, we were the right project at the wrong time."

The wrong project at the right time is the best way to sum up GODZILLA: 1985. Tauted by Toho Films as a direct sequel to the original (and conveniently ignoring the dozen or so pitiful sequels that were actually made) and the movie that would return the Godzilla mythos to some semblance of dignity; the film is finally an inferior combination of good ideas badly done and the worst elements of past films.

The story, such as it is, has Godzilla once again returning to do the Tokyo stomp before once again biting the bullet. Raymond Burr,

for old times sake, is once again on hand as intrepid reporter Steve Martin. Burr, however, had little more to do than watch the destruction on a monitor and tell the military types they don't know what they're doing.

The much publicized mechanical effects on the Godzilla head did little to detract from the fact that it's still a man in a suit (played this time by K. Satsuma). A mild approach to a revenge motive is the closest thing to real characterization in the film.

GODZILLA: 1985, like its Toho brethren, suffered massive cuts and editing before it reached these shores. An estimated 30 minutes of footage was removed; slicing away bits of characterization and special effects. The original Japanese score was edited, rearranged and, in some cases, replaced with totally unrelated music.

Calling this picture stupid would be too kind. Calling it boring would be honest.

By the mid 80's, most experts were in agreement that the simple, somewhat innocent storytelling formula made famous by KING KONG had gone by the boards. Well, nobody told the folks at Disney because if you substitute a dinosaur for the big ape and let the title creature live, you have BABY....SECRET OF THE LOST LEGEND (1985).

BABY follows a pair of scientists (William Katt and Sean Young) who discover a family of Brontosaurus living in the jungles

William Katt in "Baby . . . " (photo © Buena Vista)

of the West Indies. Everything is cozy between man and beast until a group of bad guy opportunists (led by a truly nasty Patrick McGoohan) enter the picture. They see financial possibilities in the creatures and capture a baby Sauropoda. Just when things look their darkest, the good guy scientist and the mother Brontosaurus come charging in like the cavalry, route the bad guys and the dinosaurs live happily ever after.

The story is pretty predictable stuff, but the dinosaurs, an interesting mixture of puppets, cable control and men in suits, works a lot better than one would expect. Largely harmless and mildy amusing.

PEE-WEE'S BIG ADVEN-TURE (1985) features deliberately primitive dinosaur sequences interspersed in the title character's fantasy adventure. In a dream sequence, a creaky stop motion T-Rex eats Pee-Wee's bicycle. In another, he disrupts a Japanese monster movie in the making that features Godzilla and Ghidrah.

"I guess I tend to respond to a certain level of craftsmanship and art that is not in vogue right now," said director Tim Burton in defense of the effects in PEE-WEE. "I think it's possible to be crude, funky and two-dimensional in your effects and still have them work."

The following year brought an only passable science fiction/teen comedy MY SCIENCE PROJECT (1986) that contains one very good scene in which a Tyrannosaurus comes out of the past to terrorize the present. The creature, a nifty little rod and cable puppet, was built and animated in 17 weeks by a battery of effects people headed up by John Scheele, Doug Beswick and a little known consultant by the name of Rick Baker. Given that pedigree, it's no wonder that the short life and untimely death of the creature is the only thing most people recall about the film.

Remember that mystery film that resulted in Jim Henson's dinosaur project being shelved? Well, it finally surfaced in 1989 as the Steven Spielberg-produced, Don Bluth-directed THE LAND BEFORE TIME, a cartoon adventure akin to BAMBI in which an orphaned baby dinosaur and a rag tag group of friends go on an adventure odyssey through a primeval, prehistoric world to a valley where they all live happily after after.

While producing AN AMERICAN TAIL, talk began of the next feature between Spielberg (who would ultimately co-produce with George Lucas) and Bluth. The former was interested in doing something with dinosaurs, which he saw as a popular topic with children. Spielberg's first concept, according to John Cawley's THE ANIMATED FILMS OF DON BLUTH, was to intentionally do a

"The Land Before Time" (Photos © 1988 Universal City Studios)

film like BAMBI, only with dinosaurs, achieving a dynamic similarity to the "Rite of Spring" sequence in Disney's FANTASIA. In fact, Spielberg envisioned the entire film with no dialogue. From this rough concept, the film grew to include several young dinosaurs. Eventually it was believed that it couldn't carry a storyline without dialogue.

Recalled Don Bluth, "THE LAND BEFORE TIME was actually a concept before it was a story. Spielberg said, 'Basically, I want to do a soft picture that does not have a real driving plot. It's about five little dinosaurs and how they grow up and work together as a group.' We agreed that the Tyrannosaurus Rex would be a great villain. As we talked, we decided that this would be more of a pastoral kind of picture. It needs to be symphonic in nature, soft and gentle."

The script had to be approved by a number of parties in different locations, so sections of script were approved at a time, rather than as a whole. Bluth commented that it felt like his old days at Disney, when segments were developed independently of a finished script.

"As the storyboarding continued," recalled Bluth, "we came up with another idea, that none of these dinosaurs get along with each other, they all hate each other. They're taught from the time they were born not to associate with each other. That's racism. They're going to have to be untaught the racist idea and learn to like each other, and therein lies the triumph of the movie. They would work together to overcome a common goal or enemy."

Don Bluth's cartoon work is first rate. The diversity of realistic and caricature style dinosaurs is broad enough not to be offensive to purists and, best of all, kids love it. So, for that matter, do less demanding adults.

But did Spielberg getting there first mean the end of Jim Henson's prehistoric vision? We may never know. But Bill Stout claims we almost did.

"I saw Jim a little while ago," laments Stout. "He was real excited. He said, 'The dinosaur film is on again. I'll give you more details later.'

"He died two months later."

79

"Godzilla, King of the Monsters" (courtesy of Steve Miner)

GODZILLA

"Godzilla, King of the Monsters" (courtesy of Steve Miner)

SHOWDOWN ON ALCATRAZ

"Godzilla, King of the Monsters" (courtesy of Steve Miner)

"Godzilla, King of the Monsters" (courtesy of Steve Miner)

F-16 ON MASON STREET

"Godzilla, King of the Monsters" (courtesy of Steve Miner)

"Godzilla, King of the Monsters" (courtesy of Steve Miner)

SCENE #: 207   SHOTS #: 4-7

"Godzilla, King of the Monsters" (courtesy of Steve Miner)

"Godzilla, King of the Monsters" (courtesy of Steve Miner)

"Godzilla, King of the Monsters" (courtesy of Steve Miner)

THE DESERT TREK #2   NHP

MR. SAUROLOFF'S SACRIFICE   NHP

"Natural History Project" (Art by William Stout, © 1985 Warner Brothers)

"Natural History Project" (Art by William Stout, © 1985 Warner Brothers)

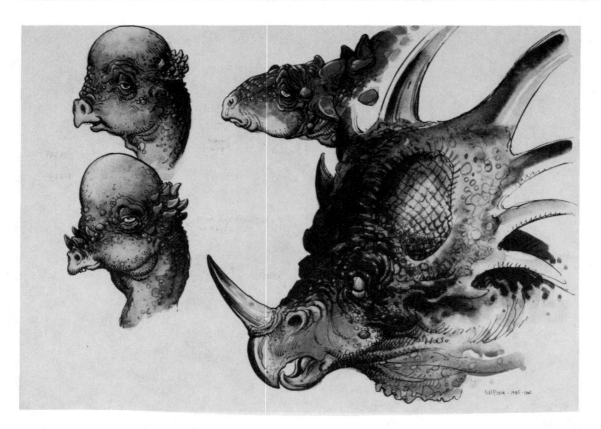

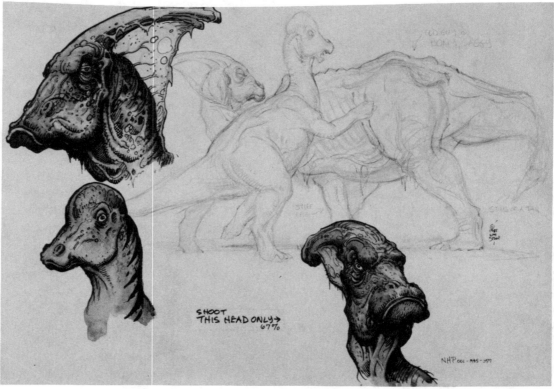

"Natural History Project" (Art by William Stout, © 1985 Warner Brothers)

"BEAUREGARD" ("Styraco") (STRACK?) NHP

"T. REX" NHP

"Natural History Project" (Art by William Stout, © 1985 Warner Brothers)

"Natural History Project" (Art by William Stout, © 1985 Warner Brothers)

"SQUEAK" ("Coru") NHP₀₁₁-₁₉₈₅-₀₉₆

"OVI" NHP₀₁₀-₁₉₈₅-₀₉₅

"Natural History Project" (Art by William Stout, © 1985 Warner Brothers)

11

Caution, Dinosaurs Ahead

You know a trend is on the horizon when Troma Pictures is on the case. And so, from the people that gave you THE TOXIC AVENGER, comes the official sign that dinosaur movies are in for the '90s with not one but two dinosaur infested movies.

WIZARDS OF THE DEMON SWORD and A NYMPHOID BARBARIAN IN DINOSAUR HELL (1991) both have a couple of things in common. They are low budget quickies that went straight to video, and they feature strange bits of casting (WIZARDS toplines Russ Tamblyn and Lyle Waggoner, while NYMPHOID features schlock babe Linda Corwin).

What these tales—WIZARDS a bit of sword and sorcery, and BARBARIAN a look at a prehistoric post-nuclear society—also feature is decent, if somewhat crude, dinosaur stop motion effects. When all is said and done, let the record show that Troma Pictures was there first, if not necessarily with the best.

CLIFFORD, the 1991 comedy starring comic Martin Short, is the first '90s big budget studio effort to have dinosaurs as featured players. Unfortunately, as with many previous efforts, this tale of a 10 year old with a dinosaur fixation takes the easy way by opting for dinos in a suit rather than the real thing. More's the pity.

Remember THE LOST WORLD, both the good one and the bad? Well, a third attempt at doing right by the Arthur Conan Doyle classic will be out sometime in 1992, retelling the time honored tale with an added twist. Tentatively titled THE LOST WORLD and RETURN TO THE LOST WORLD, these two

"A Nymphoid Barbarian in Dinosaur Hell" (Photo © 1990 Troma, Inc.)

The Flintstones head for Hollyrock (photo © 1961 Hanna-Barbera)

two-hour films, which may be re-leased to television as a four-hour miniseries, stars John Rhys Davies as Professor Challenger, and David Warner as his scientific antago-nist, Professor Summeries.

The first two hours retell the familiar LOST WORLD story in which Challenger, Summeries and intrepid reporter Ed Malone travel to the strange prehistoric plateau where they encounter dinosaurs and stone age tribes. The second film takes place years later, when our group returns to the plateau to combat a greedy industrialist in destroying the Lost World and its occupants in the name of progress. THE LOST WORLD and RETURN TO THE LOST WORLD are di-rected by Timothy Bond, and prom-ise good dinosaur effects courtesy of Image Quest, Ltd.

Tentatively (don't you just love that word?) set to go before the Disney cameras in December 1991 for a 1993 release is DINOSAURS, a big-budget prehistoric fantasy directed by stop motion pro David Allen from a Jeanne Rosenberg script. It chronicles the adventure of a prehistoric creature who joins a group of dinosaurs on a magical trip through the Valley of Plenty.

Although stop motion is Allen's forte, word has it that the wide variety of dinosaurs will involve a combination of a number of spe-cial effects.

THE FLINTSTONES are mak-ing a gradual transition from ani-mated TV series (see next chapter) to live-action feature film, and Hollyrock will never be the same.

Producer Joel Silver, screen-writer Steven de Souza and pro-posed project director Richard Donner, whose cumulative credits include COMMANDO, THE RUNNING MAN, DIE HARD, SUPERMAN, the LETHAL WEAPON trilogy and PREDATOR, are doing their best to make the continuing FLINTSTONES phenomenon a celebration that fans will remember.

"I love the idea of doing the FLINTSTONES," explains de Souza, "because I've maimed and killed all these people in the movies and this would be a change of pace. And Joel Silver and I have worked together so well in the past. I know Joel's excited about it. He's one of those guys who has all the memorabilia in his office. He has the Fred Flintstone pencil sharpener, the Wilma this, the Wilma that."

The casting of THE FLINTSTONES has been the source of a great many rumors. Insiders have claimed that Robert Redford has expressed interest in playing Fred and that Jack Nicholson wants in as well. There's also talk that Arnold Schwarzenegger is looking for a leopard skin caveman suit.

Producer Silver is having a great time fielding these pretenders to the Flintstones throne. "Nicholson? Redford? Are you kidding?" he laughs. For a time, Jim Belushi was set to play Fred, but now it seems as though ROSEANNE's John Goodman will essay the role.

De Souza adds that there have been talks with Rick Moranis about portraying Barney Rubble. "It's not set yet," the writer admits, "but I think he's a likely candidate. Vanna White from WHEEL OF FORTUNE has been campaigning to play Wilma, with her agent and managers calling the office. She has some things that would help. She's cute, she's perky, she has red hair and she's two-dimensional," he laughs. "Really, though, I think they would want a comedienne. This film may also have numerous cameos. THE FLINTSTONES is so popular that people want to have something to do with it. Remember the old shows where they would have cameos by people like Stony Curtis, Cary Granite and Ann Margrock? I wouldn't be surprised if that happens here as well."

While both Silver and de Souza are keeping the particulars of the storyline undercover for the moment, the screenwriter doesn't mind whetting appetites with a few tantalizing details.

"We decided we would do something like BOB & CAROL & TED & ALICE, only we're calling it FRED & WILMA & BARNEY & BETTY, and it will probably be rated R," de Souza deadpans. He grows silent for a moment, and the question arises as to just how serious he's being. "It's really an inclusive adventure. Barney is like Ozzie in OZZIE AND HARRIET. What did Ozzie do for a living? Nobody knows, it was never stated. But Barney, although very few people are aware of it, was supposed to be a crackpot inventor. It was dealt with in a few episodes, but then they mostly abandoned it and started going bowling or to the Buffalo Lodge. Our situation is that Barney has a good idea for an invention. Fred sees dollar signs and says, 'Let me handle this, kid,' and they get in over their heads in a giant business deal which at first promises to completely modernize Bedrock society, and ultimately threatens to destroy it."

De Souza claims that the film will be presented in the tradition of GHOSTBUSTERS, BACK TO THE FUTURE and GREMLINS. In other words, a fantasy film with a lot of action and adventure.

"It isn't going to be a simple domestic comedy," he explains. "It'll have some very spectacular things. Obviously, we're going to have to be very true to the characters because you must be careful about not undermining people's fond memories of the TV show—although I think it was innocent to a degree that wouldn't be wise today. The TV show is rated G and now, if a movie comes out rated G, no one will see it. THE FLINTSTONES will be PG. When Fred hits himself in the thumb with a hammer, will he say 'damn?' We've actually had debates over that matter. That's not to imply that the picture will be risque, but it will reflect current mores."

The film's effects will most likely be handled by The Henson Company. De Souza points out that in Bedrock, your toaster and record player, for example, would most likely be a bird.

"Those things will probably be the more traditional puppets," he explains. "The one thing that I think would be a mistake would be to use real animals. When Wilma takes a shower, an elephant would be the nozzle, but if it's a real elephant, you would fall out of the movie. Everything will have to be built at great difficulty and great expense. I'm trying not to write things that are totally impractical, but that's certainly a challenge."

One potential source of competition to THE FLINTSTONES may come from the on-again/off-again, seemingly locked in development hell, live-action version of THE JETSONS. De Souza doesn't agree.

"I don't think the characters of THE JETSONS have achieved the same pervasive popularity as THE FLINTSTONES," he observes. "Unlike the Jetsons, the Flintstones are really archetypal characters to whom everybody relates. Fred is a braggart, Barney is a dreamer, and the two women are realists. They're very traditional characters, so people can relate to them. The Jetsons, on the other hand, are more artificial in the way that the BRADY BUNCH family is artificial. Somehow, in a strange way, by attempting to be more real, it doesn't seem to strike the same inner chord with the mass consciousness.

"God," de Souza laughs. "We're getting awfully profound here talking about cartoon characters."

Dinosaurs in the '90s are bound for glory if Steven Spielberg's JURASSIC PARK has anything to do with it. Scheduled for a 1993 release, this rumored $70 million adaptation of Michael Crichton's

best selling novel, tells the story of an island resort headed up by a renegade industrialist whose scientists have discovered how to clone five dinosaurs from the DNA found in fossils.

A group of scientists and corporate raiders are invited to inspect the island prior to its opening as a big budget amusement park. But when an industrial spy attempting to steal dinosaur embyros shorts out the island's computer/security system, the dinosaurs escape and all hell breaks loose.

But don't take my word for it. Read the book and then salivate at the possibilities of the movie adaptation done right.

Word has it that that Spielberg is at least willing to put his money where his mouth is. A lion's share of the film's proposed budget is being earmarked for the construction of full sized robot dinosaurs. Academy Award winning effects man Stan Winston has expressed interest in stepping aboard the good ship JURASSIC PARK, and it has also been rumored that Ray Harryhausen will come out of retirement to serve as consultant on the epic.

Harryhausen denies the rumor, but does hold out high hopes for the film. "It's a great adventure and Steven Spielberg is more than capable of pulling it off. I can't wait."

Neither can I, because a fantastic JURASSIC PARK would be a fitting validation on more than 80 years of dinosaur filmmaking,

the good and the bad, and provides a springboard into even more fantastic journeys involving those wonderful creatures from our past, far beyond the year 2,000.

Dinosaur movies. Long may they roar.

12

Yabba Dabba Do

Television finally got wise to the importance of dinosaurs, even in a supporting role, in 1960 when the animation team of Hanna-Barbera brought THE FLINTSTONES to the small screen. But, historically speaking, THE FLINTSTONES were not the first dinosaur antics on the boob tube.

That honor, such as it is, goes to the mid-'50s TV series JUNGLE JIM. That series, which starred former Tarzan Johnny Weissmuller as a jungle explorer-crime fighter, was notorious for recycling old stock footage, so it came as no surprise that some rear projected giant lizard footage turned up in an episode in which Jim travels to a lost plateau to rescue an explorer.

Runner-up honors also go to a '50s chestnut, the anthology series SCIENCE FICTION THEATER. The episode in question told the story of a mammoth found frozen in a block of ice, thawed out and brought back to life. Given the limited budgets of the day, there was never a doubt that the creature would be friendly, not too big and doomed to an untimely death in an auto accident. Simple pulpy fun.

There was never any plans to make THE FLINTSTONES scientifically accurate. Cavemen and dinosaurs would co-exist in a blue collar world. The adventures of this modern stone age family were a not too veiled take on THE HON-EYMOONERS. However, the night time animated adventures of Fred,

Barney, Wilma and Betty (whose voices were supplied by Alan Reed, Mel Blanc, Jean Vanderpyl and Bea Benaderet) did successfully incorporate dinosaurs with definite personalities and attitudes into the show's weekly adventures.

There was man's best friend

(Dino) of course, but the main hook week after week turned out to be dinosaurs as household appliances, earth-moving machinery, cars and otherwise normally perceived inanimate objects; bitching, cracking wise and otherwise pontificating on the state of their prehistoric

The original Sleestaks in the first "Land of the Lost" (photo © 1973 Sid and Marty Krofft

world in a usually bored, often cynical manner. Sure Fred was a hoot, but give me the wit and wisdom of that dinosaur dust mop any day.

IT'S ABOUT TIME (1966-67) was a pretty dim-witted comedy set up about astronauts who travel back to the stone age and are ma-rooned. These basically sophomoric proceedings were only slightly improved with creature footage from the movie DINOSAURUS! that turned up periodically.

Series and anthology shows continued to find that getting blood out of a turnip (or in this case recycled dinosaur footage) could add spice to their productions. And it was not all mercenary in tone. Rod Serling made effective use of some brief footage from the 1925 version of THE LOST WORLD in a TWILIGHT ZONE episode in which a passenger airplane gets lost in time. At the other extreme, the ever frugal Irwin Allen managed to recycle his blatant 1960 THE LOST WORLD lizard footage into episodes of two of his series, VOYAGE TO THE BOTTOM OF THE SEA and THE TIME TUNNEL. Fortunately, Allen's two other series, LOST IN SPACE and LAND OF THE GIANTS, survived that fate.

Easily dinosaurs' finest television hour came about when Sid and Marty Krofft came up with LAND OF THE LOST (1974-77), a science fiction-adventure series that combined live action, well written stories and great stop motion animated dinosaurs into a show that was almost too good for its intended Saturday morning kid audience.

Science fiction writer David Gerrold served as story editor during LAND OF THE LOST's first season. He claims that while the Kroffts received "created by" credit, it was really his nimble fingers that knocked out the premise of forest ranger Rick Marshall (Spencer Milligan), Will (Wesley Eure) and Holly (Kathy Coleman) who, while on a river boating trip, plunge down a waterfall through a time vortex and into a prehistoric lost continent populated by dinosaurs.

"The producers had gone

Evil reptilian Sleestaks create havoc in the prehistoric world of Sid and Marty Krofft's "Land of the Lost" for ABC. (Photo © Sid and Marty Krofft.)

through a bunch of magazines, cut out pictures of dinosaurs and giant insects and they had the title LAND OF THE LOST," recalls Gerrold. "Syd told me, 'Here's the title. We have this family and they go over a waterfall into a place where there are dinosaurs.' My job was to create the characters and the story based on what they told me."

Gerrold offers that one of the things that made LAND OF THE LOST a success was the Kroffts' insistence that the dinosaurs really look like dinosaurs. Consequently, he viewed the hiring of stop motion experts Gene Warren and Gene Warren, Jr. as a step in the right direction.

"I knew their reputation was one of the being very methodical animators and that alone made it obvious that the show was putting together some technology that had never been tried on television before."

The Warren-generated dinosaurs were the result of animated models, shot and manipulated a frame at a time on table top sets, and blended with live action. Some early problems developed when the animation, shot at 24 frames per second, did not match the 60 frames per second of live action footage, giving a jittery look to the animation. The problem was solved, however, when the number of animated frames per second were increased to match the live action film speed.

Adding to the revolutionary

nature of the show was Gerrold's insistence on employing name science fiction and genre TV writers like Larry Niven, Norman Spinrad, Walter (Mr. Chekov) Koenig, Ben Bova and D.C. Fontana to pen the scripts.

"It wasn't that I went out of my way to hire science fiction writers," insists Gerrold. "It's just that they seemed to be able to work within the limits of the show while a lot of regular TV writers came up with ideas that were inappropriate. I went into that show with the attitude that I was going to hire the best writers I knew who could tell a LOST OF THE LOST kind of story."

Gerrold left the show after the first season and, to date, says he has not seen any second or third season episodes. He did   receive word of mouth that indicated second season writers managed to carry on in the tradition of the precedent setting first season. He also recalls hearing from sources that the third season, in which an uncle, Jack Marshall (Ron Harper), joins the group, took off in a totally different direction.

"I remember an episode during the first season in which Will Marshall says, 'There's got to be a reason for everything that happens here.' I was told in the third season that, in one episode, somebody said, 'Well, this is the Land of the Lost. Anything can happen here.' At that point, I knew it wasn't the same show. But overall, I would have to say that what LAND OF THE LOST attempted was largely successful."

So successful, in fact, that Sid and Marty Krofft resurrected LAND OF THE LOST late in 1991 for another run. This incarnation, starring Timothy Bottoms, Jennifer Drujan and Robert Gavin, features dinosaurs courtesy of that special effects family, The Chiodo Brothers.

Marty Krofft told STARLOG magazine, "From the beginning, our intent was to bring back a family unit similar to [the Marshalls] and put them in a similar survival situation in this strange land. We knew, however, that because this was the '90s, the sense of characters and adventures had to be more sophisticated. The bottom line is that the family is still a family, whether it's the '70s or the '90s. We also knew the main attraction would continue to be how this family adjusts to a world populated by dinosaurs....Kids and dinosaurs have always gone together. It represents a very special time in childhood when kids see the wonder in the creatures. I'm no psychologist, but my guess is that older kids and adults who tune in to LAND OF THE LOST are returning to a time that was special to them."

The late Jim Henson certainly took his fair share of looks at THE FLINTSTONES. He also obviously saw the potential for dinosaurs to carry on that stone age tradition, albeit with a more cutting edge Cretaceous attitude.

Hence the currently popular DINOSAURS, the weekly adventures of a blue collar Megalosaurus named Earl, his wife Fran, children Robbie, Charlene and Baby Sinclair, as they struggle to carve out what passes for a middle class existence in this comic age of dinosaurs.

DINOSAURS, like LAND OF THE LOST, is a TV show that is taking full advantage of the current state of special effects technology. Rather than animation, the DINOSAURS company, headed by Jim Henson's son, Brian, and Michael Jacobs, has brought the title characters to life with a mixture of state of the art puppetry and electronics shot on 35mm film.

"We are putting a lot of attention into creating this dinosaur world," states Brian Henson, who doesn't wish to go into full details regarding the way prehistoric magic is created. "To a degree it's a trade secret. But also because it distracts from what the show is about. It distracts from the world and the characters, and that's what we want to put out there. We don't want to start wowing people with screws and bolts and all sorts of junk. We want to just let people see the characters the way they are letting them believe that."

Henson adds, "Initially, [the show] was my father's idea. He had been talking about it for for a long, long time. But the show wasn't developed to any degree before he got together with Michael and together they started the development of the project. Obviously, then, I came in [and] this is the first production that we're going

into that's been developed without him. What he would think of it? I know he would love it, actually. This was—like I said—an idea of his that was always just a little too wacky and people didn't...we didn't really know how to do it, and now we can do it. And when he started it going, he realized that we were going to be able to make this.

"This really brings together several different ways he had been working," Henson continues. "It brings together some of the stuff he was doing with some of his films, and some of the stuff he did in Europe with THE STORYTELLER and DARK CRYSTAL, and brings that together with the type of entertainment from THE MUPPET SHOW and all that. It brings together a lot of his ideals onto one program."

Of the creative elements of the series, Jacobs offers, "I think that the sustenance of the show, at least the critical idea behind it, is to basically compare what might have happened had the dinosaurs evolved to what would be 1991 B.C.

Superman in the mouth of the beast (photo © Warner Brothers)

And they are great consumers. They don't know about any holes in the ozone layer. They eat and they drink and they make merry, and they abuse the world they live in much as we have. And we know the penalty that the dinosaurs paid for it, but certainly they don't know. They expect to rule this world forever. They expect that the cavemen, whom we are taking the license will exist in the time of these evolved dinosaurs....they relate to the cavemen as we relate to cows. You know, you point them out as you drive by them, but certainly you wouldn't step up to one and speak to it. So the cavemen are basically the evolving comic relief of the day. The dinosaurs are the more serious-minded adventurer characters."

Jacobs notes that the cavemen will essentially magnify the differences in evolution between the dinosaurs and where humankind is.

"For example," he smiles, "on a lunch break, Earl and Roy [dinosaurs] will glance off to see one of the cavemen banging two rocks together and getting a spark. And his mate will be looking on approvingly and in awe. And there's the spark and there's another spark and the caveman, sensing a great moment in human history, holds the rocks up, having created a spark to the heavens. And we pull the camera back and there's Earl with a Bic butane lighter and torch. So there is a difference in evolution between these two states. And we will see them. In fact, one of the things that we are having a lot of fun doing is charting the evolution of human history in front of the dinosaurs. So when you see, for example, a fellow facing down an army and the army is led by a giant, and the young boy comes out with a slingshot and fells the giant, we will see history unfold before us in time through the eyes of the dinosaurs."

DINOSAURS is a prime time ticket and so, while attempting to satisfy the kid in all of us, there is much in each week's storyline to tickle the intellect. A theme of environmental sanity and insanity makes its presence felt with surprising regularity. The characters, although reptilian, reflect human foibles at just about every turn.

Interestingly, Jacobs feels that the human audience will associate more with the dinosaur population because that will be the metaphor for what we are now than the actual human population played by human actors. He also believes that the show works in the form of subtle metaphor, quietly making commentary on our society.

"This is odd," he muses, "but when you write blatantly, you're preaching and the audience is going to turn you off because that is not what they're looking to an entertainment-based half-hour for. But if you can entertain and have an underlying message, then a) you sleep better at night, and b) you've done something because the show will be talked about the next day as to, yes, funny, and, yes, entertaining. But did you get that that's what they were trying to do? So I think that it's not going to be our headline, but I think that it's going to be underlying because it will be obvious.

"The audience will tolerate a metaphor much more than they will tolerate something thrown in their face," elaborates Jacobs. "When you—gee, I'll go back to SESAME STREET. When you watch SESAME STREET and you see the little moral lessons they are teaching children....I mean, I can tell my kids, 'No!' 'Don't!', and then these Muppets can tell my kids 'da-da-da-da,' and that's it. They sure don't learn it from me because they are being told gently, and it has spoken to them in metaphor."

Some of our greatest literature, he emphasizes, has been done in analogy and metaphorically, which is why he believes the series is better off taking that approach.

"I'll give you one quick example of a story that we [did], which is a story I love that you could not do on any other show that I've done before. We start with a tribal leader. So we'll say that this is 31 million years B.C. We'll say a million years before our series' present time. And he will be explaining that, 'I am 72 years old now, and I wish to be thrown off the cliff into the tar pit. And the reason I wish this is because I will slow the pack down when it migrates and a predator will sense me straggling and know that there is a pack of us ahead of me and fresh-kill. So what you will do is, when we turn 72 years old, you will take us and throw us off the cliff into the tar pit and it shall be a holy day, a day of solemnity, and so that that is accomplished, there will be a relative that does the hurling. And from now until time memoriala, this will be Hurling Day.'

"And then we do an optical flip forward to 30 million years B.C. and we have Earl Sinclair putting on his Sunday best, knowing that he gets to throw his mother-in-law—old lady Schneiderman—off that cliff into that tar pit—Hurling Day, which he's been looking forward to. And, in fact, you can't do a story about what we do to our elderly, and how we treat them without boring everybody. But you can have a son-in-law throwing his mother-in-law, legally, off the cliff. And you can certainly get a generation of adults watching that going, yea. But you can't do it live action. So there's where we hope that we will be entertaining and adult."

The true sense of the adult in DINOSAURS came during a first season episode in which Earl received a letter from a lawyer that stated: "My client wishes to come Thursday at noon to bite your head off and take your wife."

Dinosaurs, long on the verge of extinction, have finally made it into the 20th Century. And joined the human race.

Big, blustery megalosaures Earl Sinclair eagerly awaits the hatching of his newest family in the premiere episode of "Dinosaurs". (Photo credit Bob D'Amico/ABC © 1991 Capital Cities/ABC, Inc.

FOTO FANTASIES
DEPARTMENT I-P
POST OFFICE BOX 59
EAST MEADOW, NEW YORK 11554
(516) 542-7711

Now available by mail order: Color/Black and White photos (stills); slides, posters, brochures and specialty items.

Send for the following free lists of color slides and photos:

- Fantasy/Horror Theatrical Films (*Conan, Dawn of the Dead, Dracula*)
- Fantasy/Horror Theatrical Films #2 (*Evil Dead, Nightmare on Elm Street, Return of the Living Dead*)
- Fantasy/Horror TV
- Science-Fiction Theatrical Films #1 (*Alien, The Empire Stikes Back, Forbidden Planet*, etc.)
- Science-Fiction Theatrical Films #2 (*Road Warrior, Star Wars, Return of the Jedi*, etc.)
- SF-TV #1 (*Buck Rogers, Space: 1999, U.F.O.*, etc.)
- SF-TV #2 (*Knight Rider, Lost in Space, V*, etc.)
- Super Heroes
- Cartoons--TV & Theatrical (*Captain Harlock, Lord of the Rings, Star Blazers, Wizards*, etc.)
- James Bond (Over 500 different shots!)
- Female Stars
- Male Stars

Please enclose two (2) 29¢ stamps for each list

For other material, send specific requests along with one stamped, self-addressed business-sized (#10 long) envelope. We do not have lists on posters, brochures and specialty items. Let us know what interests you. Better yet, call.

We also buy and trade--all subjects welcome. Inquire, along with a stamped, self-addressed business-sized (#10 long) envelope. We are particularly interested in good quality color transparencies.

DEALERS: INQUIRE ABOUT WHOLESALE RATES AND TERMS